Grade **4**

Scott Foresman

The Grammar & Writing Book

ISBN: 0-328-14638-2

3 4 5 6 7 8 9 10 V008 09 08 07 06

PEARSON
Scott
Foresman

Editorial Offices: Glenview, Illinois • Parsippany, New Jersey • New York, New York
Sales Offices: Boston, Massachusetts • Duluth, Georgia • Glenview, Illinois
Coppell, Texas • Sacramento, California • Mesa, Arizona

Table of Contents

Writer's Guide

Rubrics and Models

Evaluate Your Writing

Grammar and Writing Lessons

Writing for Tests

Grammar Patrol

Index

Writer's Guide

Focus/Ideas

Good writers focus on a **main idea** and develop this idea with strong, supporting details. In addition, they know their purpose for writing. Will the writing inform, persuade, or entertain readers? Your purpose is important because it helps focus your main idea.

Even a phone message has a main idea and a purpose:

Main Idea   How and when your brother will get home

Purpose   To inform your mom

Details   Details support and develop your main idea. Your telephone note might give important information such as who is driving your brother and the exact time he is arriving. Details can also make writing lively and interesting. Compare the two sentences below.

Our dog likes candy. (lacks detail)

Our collie Shadow wags her tail wildly when she hears a candy wrapper crinkle. (adds interest)

Strategies for Focus and Ideas

- Choose a topic that you can work with. A topic such as "Famous Presidents" is too large for a one-paragraph essay.
- Choose a purpose that fits your topic. For example, a funny story would entertain readers, but an article on war might not.
- Make sure that the details you choose focus on your main idea.

A Match the number of each title with the letter of the purpose that best suits it.

A Entertain **B** Inform **C** Persuade **D** Describe

1. Why Our Town Needs a Community Center
2. My Most Embarrassing Moment
3. How Ocean Currents Affect Our Weather
4. An Interesting House in Our Neighborhood

B Read the paragraph below. Write the numbers of any sentences that do not focus on the main idea stated in the first sentence.

(5) Bermuda is a wonderful place for a vacation. **(6)** The climate is warm and sunny. **(7)** Hamilton is the capital, but St. George is the oldest settlement. **(8)** Sandy beaches and rocky coves enchant visitors. **(9)** Europeans first settled in Bermuda in 1609. **(10)** You can dive to explore sunken wrecks or skim across the smooth blue waves in a sailboat.

C Complete one of the following sentences to begin a paragraph. Then write three sentences of your own to give details about the first sentence.

My favorite place in the world is ___.
___ is the best book I ever read.
Brothers and sisters can be ___.

Improving Focus/Ideas

Original

> Many people know Cinderella from the Disney cartoon. Butterflies are like that too.
>
> A butterfly begins its life as a tiny egg. One day the egg hatches, and out crawls a baby caterpillar. Right away this little creature begins to munch on leaves. I'm not sure what kind of leaves it likes best, though. When the caterpillar is fully grown and can't eat anything else, it makes a cocoon and goes to sleep.
>
> How can a greedy, slow-moving worm turn into such a beautiful creature? Scientists may have an answer, but I don't really understand it.

Revising Tips

Use a strong, focused main idea statement.   (Revise first paragraph to lead to this main idea sentence: *No fairy tale is more magical than the life cycle of a butterfly.*)

Include all essential information.   (Add details telling how the butterfly emerges from its cocoon.)

Use only details that focus on the main idea.   (Take out *I'm not sure what kind of leaves it likes best, though.*)

Define difficult or new terms.   (Add words to help the reader understand the word *cocoon.*)

Keep your purpose in mind.   You are comparing the butterfly's story to a magical fairy tale. Keep this idea in focus by adding details that refer to magic.

Improved

You've probably heard the story of Cinderella. She's the poor girl who became a princess. Did you know that there's a Cinderella story going on in the natural world all the time? No fairy tale is more magical than the life cycle of a butterfly.

A butterfly begins its life as a tiny egg. One day the egg hatches, and out crawls a baby caterpillar. Right away this little creature begins to munch on leaves. When the caterpillar is fully grown and can't eat anything else, it winds itself up in a silky cocoon and goes to sleep. This is where the magic begins.

Something begins to happen inside the cocoon. A head bursts out, then a crumpled pair of wings. The caterpillar has become a butterfly.

How can a greedy, slow-moving worm turn into such a beautiful creature? Scientists may have an answer, but to me there is only one explanation. It's magic!

Writer's Corner

Picture your writing as a pyramid. At the top is the main idea. Keep this main idea in position with well-focused details, which form the base of the pyramid.

Organization/Paragraphs

When you write, put ideas in an order that makes sense. **Organization**—the way ideas are put together—is like the skeleton of a body. It holds things together and gives shape.

Here are some ways to organize your writing.

- a story with a beginning, middle, and end
- a comparison-contrast
- a step-by-step explanation
- a description from top to bottom

Before you begin to write, think of the best way to put your ideas together. If you are describing how two best friends are alike and different, a comparison-contrast would work. If you are telling about something that happened to you, a story form would be good.

Choosing a basic structure is only the first step in organizing your writing. You will also need to connect your ideas and make them move from beginning to end.

Strategies for Choosing a Main Idea and Purpose

- Begin paragraphs with topic sentences that tell the main idea. Use details that support that main idea.
- Tell events in the order in which they happened.
- Use sequence words such as *first*, *next*, and *finally*.
- Use connectors such as *but* and *however* to show differences and *too* and *also* to show likenesses.

A Match the number of each writing assignment below with the letter of the organization it calls for.

   A Description   **C** Comparison-contrast
   B Story   **D** Step-by-step explanation
   1. Tell how Mondays are different from Fridays.
   2. Explain how to get from the school to your house.
   3. Describe how to recognize your house.
   4. Tell something funny that happened in your family.

B Write the best word or words from the Connecting Words box to make the sentences flow smoothly. Capitalize words that begin sentences.

Connecting Words		
but	finally	first
for example	however	too

   (5) I always look forward to summer vacation. Sometimes, ___, things don't go as planned. **(6)** ___, last summer my family rented a cabin in the woods. **(7)** ___ of all, it rained nearly every day. **(8)** The mosquitoes were really bad ___. **(9)** ___, Dad said he couldn't stand it any more, and we went home. **(10)** It was not what we'd planned, ___ I did get all my summer reading done!

C Think of a task that you have to do at home. Write a step-by-step explanation describing how to do this task. Use order words such as *first*, *next*, *now*, and *finally*.

Improving Organization Paragraphs

Original

Once my mom came home and was mad because Dad and I were making brownies. She said that this was how not to bake brownies. We found out the hard way. What we did was forget to turn on the oven and to add baking powder. I found a recipe, but several of the ingredients weren't in the house. We splattered lots of batter on the walls when we were using the electric mixer. Eggshells got in the batter, and flour spilled all over the floor. I left the kitchen and waited for Mom to return.

Revising Tips

Organize your writing around your main idea. (Focus the story. For example, you could introduce it as a step-by-step recipe for *how not to bake brownies*.)

Use an order that makes sense. (Describe events in the order that they occurred: finding recipe, mixing, cooking, and so on.)

Use sequence words. Sequence words will help make the order clear. (*First find a brownie recipe. . .; Then spill flour over the floor. . .; Next break two eggs. . .*)

Start a new paragraph when the topic shifts. (This story could have an introductory paragraph, paragraphs about mixing and cooking, and a conclusion.)

Write a conclusion that wraps up your ideas. (Return to your main idea of *how not to bake brownies*.)

Improved

Would you like to learn how <u>not</u> to bake brownies? I can tell you because one day Dad and I found out the hard way. Here's our step-by-step method.

First find a brownie recipe with several ingredients you don't have in the house. Then spill flour all over the floor. Next break two eggs into the bowl and accidentally drop the shells in too. Finally, make sure to forget the baking powder. Beat up all the ingredients with an electric mixer, and splatter lots of the batter on the walls.

When you are ready to bake the brownies, it is important not to turn on the oven. Remember, you don't want the brownies to cook.

Leave the kitchen and wait for your mom to return. She will let you know that this is how not to bake brownies.

Writer's Corner

Reading a well-organized piece of writing is like going on a trip. Be sure you come back to where you started from at the end. Make your end a little different, though—you did learn something on your trip!

Voice

Voice is the *you* that comes through in your writing and makes it interesting. Writers with a strong voice engage their readers and speak directly to them. Voice shows that the writer knows a topic and cares about it.

- As a baby, I didn't like asparagus. (weak voice)
- I used to cry in my highchair as I pushed slimy green asparagus off my plate. It looked like snakes. (strong voice)

Strategies for Developing Your Voice

- Know your purpose and audience. A story about a funny event written to a friend should have a light, playful voice. A research paper for your teacher should have a serious, well-informed voice.
- Elaborate on your ideas with words that match your voice. Use words such as *should*, *best*, and *most important* in persuasive writing. Informal language, perhaps exaggeration or even slang, suits a friendly, casual voice. Business letters need a serious, objective voice and precise words. Depending on your message, your voice might also be humorous, angry, excited, or sarcastic.
- Remember that all good writing needs a voice to hold a reader's interest. Voice should be engaging, lively, and interesting. Let your readers know how you feel.

A Match the numbered item with the type of writing it is.

A Mystery story
B Amusing article
C Note to a friend
D Letter to the newspaper

1. Something must be done about the litter on the streets and sidewalks of our town.
2. Hal froze in terror when the light dimmed and the door behind him creaked on its hinges.
3. You wouldn't believe the stuff I got for Halloween.
4. If your idea of fun is eating mud, you'd probably enjoy dinner with some of my relatives.

B Match each kind of voice with the writing it fits best.

A Humorous   B Angry   C Friendly   D Serious

5. A letter to your aunt about a great day at the beach
6. A story about a cat that loves to take baths
7. An editorial criticizing campers who leave their campfires unattended
8. An article about the discovery of a new dinosaur

C Choose one of the following opening sentences. Add sentences to write a paragraph about the topic. Use a voice that fits your main idea and audience.

We all benefit by taking better care of the environment.

Some foods make me gag just thinking about them.

Improving Voice

Original

My family owns a cat named Bender that displays most unusual behavior patterns. Much of the time he adopts the habits of a dog. Bender comes when one calls his name, and he wags his tail when he is happy. On outings, Bender walks on a leash like a dog. Bender also attempts to retrieve tennis balls by rolling them forward with his paws.

Strangely, Bender's voice has changed in the last few months. The sound he now makes is very different from a typical cat's meow. Bender may be taking the final step to becoming a dog by learning how to bark.

Revising Tips

Match your language to your purpose.   This is a funny story. Use an informal, humorous voice to bring it to life.

Use appropriate words.   (A phrase such as *displays most unusual behavior patterns* is too formal for a funny story. *Our cat Bender thinks he's a dog* works better.)

Elaborate with precise details.   (*A short, low-pitched noise* paints a much clearer picture than *the sound*.)

Get involved with your subject.   Good writers engage their readers. (Ask your readers a question: *Have you ever seen a cat retrieve a tennis ball? No?*)

Improved

Our cat Bender thinks he's a dog. He comes when you call his name, and he wags his tail when he's happy. When Bender goes outside, he walks on a leash just like "other" dogs. Have you ever seen a cat retrieve a tennis ball? No? Well, you haven't seen Bender. The only trouble is, Bender can't hold the ball in his mouth. His solution is to roll it back to you with his front paws.

Bender's meow has changed too. Now when he opens his mouth, he lets out a short, low-pitched noise like nothing you've ever heard from an animal. My dad says that Bender is taking the final step in becoming a dog. He's teaching himself how to bark!

Writer's Corner

Establish your voice at the beginning of your writing. Engage your readers by communicating, "I've got something to tell you, and it's important (or funny, or something you may disagree with)."

Word Choice

Have you noticed that good writers choose their **words** carefully? Strong verbs, exact nouns, and vivid adjectives help writers elaborate on their ideas. Well-chosen words make writing clear and lively.

- Kids don't like that dog because of the fact that he's mean. (dull and wordy)
- Kids scream when Rex snarls and lunges on his leash. (lively)

Strategies for Improving Word Choice

- Use specific nouns. (*canary* instead of *bird*, *ballerina* instead of *dancer*)
- Use strong verbs. (*wriggle* instead of *move*, *splinter* instead of *break*)
- Appeal to the senses. (*My teeth are chattering* instead of *I am cold*; *hair looks like spun gold* instead of *hair looks pretty*)
- Consider rewriting sentences that use *is, was, were, am,* and *are.* (*My stomach churned* instead of *I was sick*)
- Replace words such as *nice, great, thing,* and *stuff* with exact words. (*I collect coins and stamps* instead of *I collect things*)
- Get rid of wordiness. (*because* instead of *due to the fact that*)

Choose the word that is more vivid or exact to complete each sentence. Write the sentence.

1. The (bird, eagle) plunged down from the sky onto the rabbit.
2. We (wandered, went) slowly through the town.
3. Principal Jones (came, marched) angrily into the room.
4. The winner waved and gave a (nice, radiant) smile.
5. Al (mumbled, said) a few words into the receiver.
6. Samantha (walked, paced) restlessly backstage.

B Replace an underlined word with a word or words from the box. Rewrite the sentences.

ambled	beaklike	clamped	heaved
munched	relieved	spinach	tortoise

(7) The enormous <u>animal</u> stuck out his head and opened his eyes. (8) His vast shell <u>went</u> up and down as he approached. (9) I nervously held out some <u>food</u>. (10) Slowly he opened his <u>strange</u> mouth. (11) His jaws <u>came</u> down on the leaves. (12) He <u>ate</u> slowly for a few seconds. (13) Then he <u>went</u> away. (14) I was <u>glad</u> he had not eaten my finger.

C Write a description of a pet or a wild animal that interests you. Use vivid words that appeal to the senses.

Improving Word Choice

Original

Early summer evenings in the woods are never quiet. They are very noisy with the sounds of nature. At sunset hundreds of frogs make very high sounds. Soon after dark a bird starts to sing with certain sounds. As the moon comes up, you can hear coyotes call. Even from a distance their scary noise can make a person nervous and make a dog wake up and growl because the sound is so scary.

Late at night, when things quiet down, a sound from the river shows that other animals are around. After that, you can hear a passing duck and its very strange call.

Revising Tips

Use precise nouns.   (For example, replace *bird* with *whippoorwill*. Replace *duck* with *loon*. Replace *sounds* with more specific nouns.)

Replace weak verbs with strong ones.   (Replace *comes* with *floats*. Replace *call* with *yelp and wail*.)

Appeal to your reader's senses.   (Substitute *raise the hair at the back of your neck* for *make a person nervous*.)

Replace dull modifiers with vivid ones.   (Replace *certain* with *lonely*. Replace *very strange* with *wild, weird*.)

Avoid wordiness.   (Drop *because the sound is so scary* from last sentence of first paragraph.)

Improved

Early summer evenings in the woods of western Maine are never quiet. They come alive with the sounds of nature. At sunset hundreds of tiny frogs peep shrilly from the marsh. Soon after dark a whippoorwill repeats its lonely cry, like a tormented ghost. As the full moon floats above the white pines, coyotes yelp and wail at the sky. Even from a distance their haunting howls can raise the hair at the back of your neck and change a sleepy dog into a snarling wolf.

Late at night, when the quiet forest seems finally at rest, a splash from the river signals that beavers are once again building. Just when peace has returned, a passing loon pierces the quiet with its wild, weird laughter.

Writer's Corner

Be on the lookout for "wow" words that make writing come alive: *frothy, drizzle, plop, lurk, ripple, slurp, gritty*. Keep a notebook handy to record these words.

Sentences

Good writing flows smoothly. It is a pleasure to read aloud. Different lengths and kinds of **sentences** create a rhythm and style.

Here are some ways to improve your sentences.

- Vary sentence length. Avoid having all short sentences.
- Vary kinds of sentences. An interrogative, imperative, or exclamatory sentence can add excitement.
- Use different beginnings. Too many sentences beginning with *I*, *he*, or *the* make for a dull style.
- Use connectors. Words such as *first, but, and, although*, and *while* make sentences flow smoothly. Do not join too many sentences with *so* or *because*.

Strategy for Improving Your Sentences

Number each sentence of your writing. Make a chart like this.

Sentence number	Number of words	First word	Type of sentence (Interrogative, Declarative, Imperative, Exclamatory)	Connector words

Filling out your chart may reveal areas to improve. You may learn that you write mostly short sentences starting with *the* or that you use *so* to string too many ideas together. When you revise, try to improve these areas.

A Combine these short, choppy sentences. Use the connector provided. Write the sentences.

Example He arrived late. The car broke down. (because)

He arrived late because the car broke down.

1. We wanted to go swimming. It was too cold. (but)

2. Al won the race. He hadn't practiced. (although)

3. I sneaked out. Marilou was singing. (while)

4. We all ordered ice cream. It was so hot. (because)

B In the paragraph below, rearrange words in each sentence so that it does not begin with *I*. Start with the underlined word or phrase. Write the paragraph.

Example I went to the zoo <u>last Saturday</u>.

Last Saturday I went to the zoo.

(5) I want to become an astronaut <u>one day</u>. **(6)** I will <u>then</u> fly to all the planets. **(7)** I might discover a new planet <u>at the far end of the solar system</u>. **(8)** I could live there <u>for a few years</u> and rule a great empire. **(9)** I would <u>finally</u> return to Earth to write about my adventures. **(10)** I might become President of the United States <u>after that</u>!

C Write a description of something you really like doing. Include one interrogative and one exclamatory sentence. Start each sentence with a different word.

Improving Sentences

Original

Not everyone believes in super powers. I do. This is because of my friend Bob. He may look like an ordinary person. He possesses an amazing gift. He has a great power. He has the power to be happy under all circumstances. He is fun to be with. This is a wonderful gift.

Sometimes plans go wrong. Bob has fun anyway. It might rain during a picnic or a parade. Bob still finds a way to laugh. We didn't have enough money to go to a movie one day, so Bob decided we would put on a play instead, and we rehearsed all afternoon and put on a show that evening, and it was much more fun than a movie.

Some people have power. Happiness is more important.

Revising Tips

Use different beginnings.   (Reword some sentences beginning with *He*.)

Join choppy sentences with connecting words.
(Combine opening sentences of second paragraph to *Sometimes plans go wrong, but Bob has fun anyway.*)

Break down long stringy sentences.   (Rewrite sentence *We didn't have enough money. . .* as three sentences.)

Vary sentence types.   (Rewrite opening to include interrogative and imperative sentences.)

Improved

Do you believe in super powers? I do. Take my friend Bob, for example. He may look like an ordinary person, but he possesses an amazing gift. You see, Bob has a great power—the power to be happy under all circumstances. No matter what happens, Bob is fun to be with. What a wonderful gift this is!

Sometimes plans go wrong, but Bob has fun anyway. If it rains during a picnic or a parade, Bob still finds a way to laugh. One day we didn't have enough money to go to a movie, so Bob decided we would put on a play instead. After rehearsing all afternoon, we put on a show that evening. It was much more fun than any movie.

Bob isn't super strong physically, but he has the power to create happiness.

Writer's Corner

After you have written a first draft, ask yourself, "How could I say that differently?" Experiment with different kinds and lengths of sentences. Read your different versions aloud and choose the one that sounds most effective.

Conventions

Conventions are the rules for written language. They are signals that help readers understand writing. For example, sentences begin with capital letters and end with punctuation. Paragraphs are indented. Grammar and spelling follow patterns.

- Me and willie ax mama aunt belle and max the question we didn't get a answr. (weak conventions)
- Willie and I asked Mama, Aunt Belle, and Max the question. We didn't get an answer. (strong conventions)

Strategies for Conventions of Writing

- Use a dictionary or spell checker to check spelling.
- Make sure sentences are complete, with correct capitalization and punctuation.
- Check that subjects and verbs agree.
- Make sure you have used the correct forms of pronouns, especially pronouns that are compound subjects or objects.
- Make sure you haven't changed verb tenses by mistake.
- Check the use of apostrophes in possessive nouns and contractions.

Proofreading Marks

¶ New paragraph
≡ Capital letter
/ Lowercase letter
○ Correct the spelling.
∧ Add something.
℮ Remove something.

A Choose the correct answer and write each sentence.

1. The trophies went to Jake, Trina, and (me, I).
2. They look good, but (there, they're) really plastic.
3. Trina has (broke, broken) hers already.
4. I (do'nt, don't) know where to display mine.
5. Jake and (I, me) will compete again next year.

B Match the letter with the mistake in each sentence.

A Correct subject-verb agreement.

B End sentence with a question mark.

C Correct a misspelling.

D Add an apostrophe.

E Change a capital letter to lowercase.

(6) What do you picture when you hear the word *cat.* **(7)** Many of us visualizes a furry animal snoozing on the sofa. **(8)** Well, that's one side of a cat, but its not the whole picture. **(9)** Cats are also skilled Predators that can survive in the wild. **(10)** There's more to that sleepy bundel of fur than meets the eye!

C Write four sentences about one of the topics below. Watch your grammar, punctuation, capitalization, and spelling. Exchange papers with a partner and proofread.

A place I would like to visit

A person I would like to meet

A thing I would like to do

Improving Conventions

Original

> Our neighbor, Mr. James, plays bassoon in the Springfield symphony orchestra. Do you know what a bassoon is. I didnt until I went to hear the Orchestra give a childrens concert! There was Mr. James in the middel of the orchestra. Playing an instrument that looked like a long brown tube. The sound he made was low and melow, like a man singing. after the concert my mom and me went Backstage to meet Mr. James. His bassoon was way to big for me to hold but he said that in two years my hands would have grew. And that he would give me a lesson.

Revising Tips

Check capitalization.   Capitalize first words of sentences and proper nouns. Do not capitalize common nouns. (For example, replace *Backstage* with *backstage*.)

Look for misspellings.   (*middle* instead of *middel*; *mellow* instead of *melow*; *too* instead of *to*)

Make sure you have used punctuation, including apostrophes, correctly.   (For example, add question mark after second sentence; replace *didnt* with *didn't*.)

Check for correct pronoun usage.   (*my mom and I* instead of *my mom and me*)

Check for correct verb forms.   (*grown* instead of *grew*)

Make sure sentences are complete.   (For example, join *Playing an instrument . . .* to the sentence before it.)

Improved

Our neighbor, Mr. James, plays bassoon in the Springfield Symphony Orchestra. Do you know what a bassoon is? I didn't until I went to hear the orchestra give a children's concert. There was Mr. James in the middle of the orchestra playing an instrument that looked like a long brown tube. The sound he made was low and mellow, like a man singing. After the concert my mom and I went backstage to meet Mr. James. His bassoon was way too big for me to hold, but he said that in two years my hands would have grown. He said he would give me a lesson then.

Writer's Corner

A good proofreader is a detective. Look closely for mistakes. Here are some tricks to catch errors. Start reading in the middle of your work. Then go back and read the first part. Use a ruler to go line by line. Read your work aloud.

Rubrics and Models

Narrative Writing *Scoring Rubric*

A scoring **rubric** can be used to judge a piece of writing. A rubric is a checklist of traits, or writing skills, to look for. See pages 2–25. Rubrics give a number score for each trait.

Score	4	3	2	1
Focus/Ideas	Excellent narrative focused on a clear main idea; much elaboration	Good narrative mostly focused on a main idea; some elaboration	Sometimes unfocused narrative with unrelated details	Rambling narrative with unrelated details
Organization/ Paragraphs	Strong beginning, middle, and end, with appropriate order words	Adequate beginning, middle, and end, with some order words	May lack direction from beginning to end, with few order words	Lacks beginning, middle, end; incorrect or no order words
Voice	Writer involved—personality evident	Reveals personality at times	Little writer involvement	Careless writing with no feeling
Word Choice	Vivid, precise words that bring story to life	Adequate words to bring story to life	Few vivid or interesting words	Vague, dull, or misused words
Sentences	Excellent variety of sentences; natural rhythm	Varied lengths, styles; generally smooth	Simple, awkward, or wordy sentences; little variety	Choppy; many incomplete or run-on sentences
Conventions	Excellent control; few or no errors	No serious errors to affect understanding	Weak control; errors affect understanding	Many errors that may prevent understanding

Following are four models that respond to a prompt. Each model has been given a score, based on the rubric.

Writing Prompt Write about the first time you did something that you found interesting, exciting, or scary. Be sure your narrative has a beginning, middle, and end. Use vivid words to help readers see and feel what you experienced.

Narrative Writing Model *Score 4*

"You stick the hook through the worm? Yuck!"

It was my first time fishing. I was dying to catch a fish, but I didn't want to kill a poor little worm.

"Worms don't have feelings," Dad argued. My brothers said I was a sissy. Nothing they said could change my mind.

In the end, Dad gave me cheese from a sandwich. "Try that," he said, "but you won't catch anything."

He was wrong. A few minutes later a huge trout came flipping and flopping into the boat at the end of my line.

I caught the only fish that day. Anyone knows fish don't like worms!

Focus/Ideas Focused on the fishing experience; supported with lively details

Organization/Paragraphs Strong beginning and end; events in order and broken into paragraphs; connectors *(In the end, A few minutes later)* move story along

Voice Expresses lively humor and personality *(Anyone knows fish don't like worms!)*

Word Choice Precise word choice *(argued, trout)*; vivid imagery *(flipping and flopping)*; lively dialogue

Sentences Variety of sentence kinds and lengths

Conventions No errors

Narrative Writing Model *Score 3*

I was scared when I tried out for little league. All the other kids looked really good.

The coach put me in the outfield. I like to play infield better. I stood out there a really long time. Then a ball came my way. I lunged and stuck up my glove and cauht the ball. "Nice play" the coach yelled.

He told me to bat. I swung at a low pitch and I swung at a good pitch and then I hit one really hard up the middel.

The coach clapped his hands and I ran to first. I'm a really fast runner. He told me I'd made the team. I was so glad I jumped up and down.

Focus/Ideas   Main idea of trying out for Little League clear; a few details off the topic

Organization/Paragraphs   Clear beginning, middle, and end; good paragraphing; more connecting words needed

Voice   Writer's feelings clear (*I was scared; I was so glad I jumped up and down*)

Word Choice   Exact verbs (*lunged, yelled, clapped*) and phrases (*stuck up my glove*); overuse of *really*

Sentences   Mostly clear; one stringy

Conventions   comma errors; capitalization error (*little league*); a few spelling errors (*cauht, middel*)

Narrative Writing Model *Score 2*

> Me and my friend Bill took the bus to the square alone. We new how much we had to pay we new where to get off. We had fun on the bus. An old man told us to stop shouting and sit down. Bill wants to get pice of piza and I want to get some ice cream so we get both. It was really good. I had a sunday with hot fudj on it. We walked home. Because we didn't have any money left over for the bus.

Focus/Ideas   Shifts from experience of taking bus to what narrator and friend did on arrival; significance of event not made clear through details

Organization/Paragraphs   Opening weak; moves in order of events; no sequence words; no paragraphing

Voice   Writer's enthusiasm apparent in spite of poor control

Word Choice   Limited, dull word choice (*get, good*)

Sentences   Simple, with little variety; some long, stringy sentences

Conventions   Many misspellings; omitted word (*get pice of piza*); pronoun error (*Me and my friend Bill*); shifts in verb tense; run-on and fragment

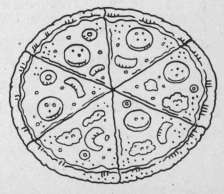

Narrative Writing Model *Score 1*

> I dident like all the noys at the pool but my mom sed I had to go and want to swim. The watter is deep it is not to cold when I put in my foot to feel it. My big sister meg is there to she is older and she can swim. She is in hih school. A real good diver to. She use to be afrade of the watter but not me I like to stand in the water and I can walk like I am swiming. There are bigger waves in the see. Mom says we will go to the cape in the sumur so then I can go swiming in the see. In the big waves.

Focus/Ideas Main idea unclear; focus shifts from pool to narrator's sister to swimming in the sea

Organization/Paragraphs Little sense of time order; weak beginning and ending

Voice Writer's feelings expressed; errors detract from sense of writer's personality

Word Choice Limited, dull word choice (*big, is*)

Sentences Little sentence variety; faulty structure

Conventions Fragments (*A real good diver to; In the big waves*); run-ons; many misspellings; verb tense errors; capitalization error (*meg*)

Descriptive Writing *Scoring Rubric*

Score	4	3	2	1
Focus/Ideas	Excellent description with clear main idea and strong, elaborated details	Good description with adequate details focused on main idea	Some descriptive details; some focus on main idea	Little focus on described subject; lacks details
Organization/ Paragraphs	Details arranged in clear order; strong beginning and ending	Details mostly arranged in order; good beginning and ending	Details not well connected; poor beginning and ending	No organization of details; lack of beginning or ending
Voice	Strong personality; clear connection between writer and subject	Writer involved; some connection between writer and subject	Writer lacking involvement; few feelings shown	Writer involvement, point of view missing
Word Choice	Specific, vivid language that appeals to several senses	Accurate, engaging language that appeals to one or two senses	Uninteresting language; little appeal to senses	Limited, vague language; repetitive
Sentences	Superior structure; excellent flow	Some varied beginnings; well constructed	Simple structures; little variety	Many errors; awkward; hard to read
Conventions	Excellent control; few or no errors	No serious errors to affect understanding	Weak control; errors that affect understanding	Many errors that prevent understanding

Following are four models that respond to a prompt. Each model has been given a score, based on the rubric.

Writing Prompt   Describe a place you know and like. It might be a favorite vacation spot, the local playground, or a corner of your backyard. Use exact words to help readers see, hear, taste, smell, and feel what you are describing.

Descriptive Writing Model *Score 4*

Do you have a place to go when you are sad or lonely? I escape to a corner of my bedroom behind a big old armchair. It is so hidden away that no one knows I'm there. I call it the Peaceful Place.

The floor of the Peaceful Place is covered with a silky-smooth old fur coat that my grandma used to wear. A photograph of my cat hangs on the wall in a silver frame. A little yellow lamp glows like the sun and gives me light.

The Peaceful Place is so quiet that I can almost hear my heart beating. When I sit there on the smooth fur in the golden light, I start to feel better right away.

Focus/Ideas   Excellent focus on the Peaceful Place with many supporting details

Organization/Paragraphs   Effective introduction and conclusion; good details in body paragraph

Voice   Clearly communicates feelings about this corner

Word Choice   Vivid word choice *(escape, hidden away)* and sensory images *(silky-smooth, glows like the sun, I can almost hear my heart beating)*

Sentences   Clear sentences of various kinds and lengths, including opening question

Conventions   No errors

Descriptive Writing Model *Score 3*

Our camp in Wisconsin is my favoret place. It is in the woods on the edge of a small river. Every summer my family goes there for two weeks.

The camp is made of logs, and, it's windows are all covered with screens. On cold nights we get shivery, but, it always get warm in the day. The cool river is mostly calm and good for swimming, and, I play ball with my dad in a farmer's field. There are farms around, they raise cows.

I like going to our camp in the peaceful and beautiful woods. Dad says he is going to make it bigger next year.

Focus/Ideas   Mostly focused on description of camp, but wanders in body paragraph

Organization/Paragraphs   Good paragraphing; effective introduction, but conclusion starts new subject

Voice   Writer's appreciation of the camp clear

Word Choice   Some phrases that appeal to senses *(shivery, cool river, peaceful and beautiful woods)*

Sentences   Some variety in kind and length

Conventions   Extra comma in compound sentences; run-on sentence; agreement error *(it always get)*; a few spelling errors *(favoret, it's)*

Descriptive Writing Model *Score 2*

The libary is my best place because it has lots of computers and I can use them all afternoon so my mom doesnt scream at me for being on the computer. Sometimes the people in the libary scream at my friends and I for talking thouh. The libary has lots of books and a slippery wooden floor, there is also a door with an alarm that goes off if you try to open it. I went threw it and get really scared when the bell goes off really loud so I use the right door now.

In conclushun I like the libary alot but mainly because of the computers and not the books.

Focus/Ideas   Mostly focused on library with many details; some elaboration off-topic

Organization/Paragraphs   Organization generally weak; attempts a conclusion

Voice   Tone enthusiastic but weakened by errors and organizational problems

Word Choice   Some vivid sensory words *(scream, slippery)*; some dull, repetitive words *(really, lots of)*

Sentences   Mostly grammatical, but loose and stringy

Conventions   Many misspellings; pronoun error *(my friends and I)*; change in verb tense *(get really scared when the bell goes off)*; run-on sentence

Descriptive Writing Model *Score 1*

The bech is where I want to go becoz my dad has a bech bugy and you can go fast over doons and swim in there when there is no school. I got sunburn last year, I codnt swim and I was to sore so my brother and me play cards inside and I win becoz my brother duznt no the names of the cards and I cod all ways win. And you can make casels out of sand to. Which is woshd away by the oshen.

Focus/Ideas   Focus mainly on beach with some descriptive details; strays into story of card game

Organization/Paragraphs   No logical order after opening; ends abruptly

Voice   Tone lively but confused

Word Choice   Limited word choice; little appeal to the senses; wordy

Sentences   Long, straggly sentences; not enough control for any variety in sentence types

Conventions   Many misspellings and comma errors; pronoun error *(my brother and me)*; omission of apostrophes for contractions; run-on and fragment; verb tense change; no paragraph indent

Persuasive Writing *Scoring Rubric*

Score	4	3	2	1
Focus/Ideas	Excellent persuasive essay with clearly stated opinion and strong elaboration	Clear opinion supported by mostly persuasive reasons	Opinion not clearly stated; weak reasons or not enough reasons	Weak or missing stated opinion; details not focused on topic
Organization/ Paragraphs	Strong, convincing introduction; reasons presented in order of importance	Interesting introduction; reasons in order of importance	Weak or unclear introduction; reasons not clear or not in order of importance	No introduction; few reasons; order not logical
Voice	Concerned, committed writer behind words	Some sense of caring, concerned writer behind words	Little sense of writer involvement with essay	No sense of writer's personality or feelings evident
Word Choice	Effective use of persuasive words	Use of persuasive words adequate to good	Few persuasive words used in essay	No persuasive words used in essay
Sentences	Varied sentence structures; excellent flow and rhythm	Some varied sentence structures; few sentence errors	Limited to simple sentence structures; some errors	Simple, choppy sentences; fragments and run-ons
Conventions	Control of all mechanical aspects of writing	Few errors in grammar, spelling, punctuation	Some distracting mechanical errors	Many errors that prevent understanding

Following are four models that respond to a prompt. Each model has been given a score, based on the rubric.

Writing Prompt   Think about something you would like to improve in your community—in your neighborhood, your school, or the whole town or city. Write a letter to the editor of your local newspaper. Persuade newspaper readers that this improvement is necessary.

Persuasive Writing Model *Score 4*

Dear Sir or Madam:

    Why is there a new "Skating Prohibited" sign at Silver Lake? I really think this is unnecessary.

    People have been skating on Silver Lake for centuries. It is peaceful, without the crowds and music of indoor rinks.

    I know the Town Council is worried about safety, but no one has drowned here in over 20 years. People have always used common sense. If the councilors want to take action, they can notify us when the ice is thick enough. A green flag means "safe," and a red flag means "unsafe."

    The people of Springfield love Silver Lake in both summer and winter. We should be able to skate on it.

                  Yours truly,
                  Thomas Kim

Focus/Ideas Focused, well supported ideas

Organization/Paragraphs Good opening and closing; information given in body paragraphs

Voice Strong voice indicating commitment to opinion

Word Choice Words persuasive (*unnecessary, should*) and specific (*A green flag means "safe"*)

Sentences Varied sentences with good rhythms

Conventions No errors; correct letter format

Persuasive Writing Model *Score 3*

Dear Sir or Madam:

 I have a great idea for that land on elm street where McCue's garage used to be. We should turn it into a garden.

 People like to grow vegetables but they don't always have room for gardens in their backyards. Gardening is fun and good exercise and it is also a way to supply nutrishous food. The goverment says we should eat nine servings of fruit and vegetables a day. My friends and I measured the McCue's sigt for a class project and the town could make at least 30 garden plots so that's a lot of vegetables.

 A community garden would be a great thing for our town.

Yours truly,

Kendra Koumjian

Focus/Ideas   Focused except for one sentence

Organization/Paragraphs   Good introduction and conclusion; logical organization of details

Voice   Believable, enthusiastic voice

Word Choice   Generally effective; some persuasive words *(a great idea, should, good exercise, great thing)*

Sentences   Several stringy sentences

Conventions   Missing commas; spelling errors; capitalization error *(elm street)*; correct letter format

Persuasive Writing Model *Score 2*

There are a lot of things that are good about this town. One thing that is'nt good is that we don't have a place for kids to go and hang out. We need a place with a gym for basketball and a pool to and we need a place where us kids can get things to eat like burgers and pizza. Pizza costs a lot at Art's pizza. It is good but still why pay all that mony. Lots of towns have a boys and girls club wher kids can hang out and get off the streets. Becaus people get mad when kids hang out on the streets. A place just for kids would be a cool thing.

William Santoro

Focus/Ideas   Generally focused; reasons could be better developed; irrelevant detail about cost of pizza

Organization/Paragraphs   Introduction in need of better focus; no paragraph indent

Voice   Feelings about topic communicated

Word Choice   Limited, dull word choice *(place, get, things, a lot, lots of)*; wordiness; slang *(hang out, cool)*

Sentences   Awkward and stringy sentences

Conventions   Sentence fragment; missing punctuation *(commas, question mark)*; contraction error *(is'nt)*; missing apostrophes *(boys and girls club)*; pronoun error *(us kids)*; misspellings; lacks greeting and closing

Persuasive Writing Model *Score 1*

Dear Sir or madam,

    Dogs have to get exersize just like us, dogs can't run when they are on a leash so we should be able to let dogs go running without a leash in the parks and woods. People would pick up after the dogs if there was sines saying pick up after dogs unless they talked another language and couldn't understand. My dog is a kind called a labrador. He loves to run off the leash, my dog is good and I clean up after it when we walk and always carry two bags just in case. My brother doesn't walk Sam until dad says not to always make me do the work.

                    Jenny Sams

Focus/Ideas   Request for relaxing of leash law not clearly stated; few focused reasons; many details off the subject

Organization/Paragraphs   Reasons not organized; no transitions; no conclusion

Voice   Identifiable voice

Word Choice   Limited word choice; wordy (*My dog is a kind called a labrador*); use of persuasive word *should*

Sentences   Rambling

Conventions   Misspellings; run-ons; faulty subject-verb agreement (*if there was sines*); capitalization errors; no closing

Expository Writing *Scoring Rubric*

Score	4	3	2	1
Focus/Ideas	Excellent explanation; main idea developed with strong details	Good explanation of main idea; details that mostly support it	Some focus on main idea; few supporting details	Main idea unfocused or lacking; few supporting details
Organization/ Paragraphs	Main idea in clear topic sentence; details in time order; appropriate connecting words	Adequate topic sentence; most details in correct order; some connecting words	Topic sentence, important details missing or in wrong order; few connecting words	No clear order to details or connecting words; no clear topic sentence
Voice	Engaging, but serious	Mostly serious, but with some inappropriate shifts	Voice not always appropriate to subject matter	Voice lacking or inappropriate
Word Choice	Topic conveyed through specific, vivid language	Topic portrayed with clear language	Some vague, repetitive, or incorrect words	Dull language; very limited word choices
Sentences	Well-crafted, varied sentences	Accurate sentence construction; some variety	Little variety; overly simple constructions; some errors	Many fragments, run-ons; sense hard to follow
Conventions	Excellent control of all mechanical aspects of writing	Few mechanical errors	Some distracting mechanical errors	Many errors that prevent understanding

Following are four models that respond to a prompt. Each model has been given a score, based on the rubric.

Writing Prompt   Choose a city you have visited or would like to visit. Write a paragraph that includes some important facts about the city. For example, you might tell about its history, important buildings, or places to visit.

Expository Writing Model *Score 4*

In Ottawa, the capital city of Canada, there are many interesting things to do and see. A good place to start a tour is Parliament Hill. From there visitors can see the river and the beautiful green-roofed Parliament buildings. Visitors who come in winter can skate on the Rideau Canal or watch dog-sled racing. They can also try the delicious fried dough that Canadians call "beaver tails." In spring, Ottawa comes alive with thousands of tulips. These are sent from Holland to thank Canadians for helping the Dutch during World War II. In summer, visitors can hike and fish in the lakes and parks. Ottawa has something to offer in every season.

Focus/Ideas   Focused on the topic of visiting Ottawa; supported with relevant facts and details

Organization/Paragraphs   Clear topic sentence; logical arrangement of details; connecting words help movement (*From there, In spring, In summer*)

Voice   Informed and caring voice

Word Choice   Precise word choice and images (*green-roofed Parliament buildings, "beaver tails," thousands of tulips*)

Sentences   Clear, varied sentences

Conventions   Excellent control; no errors

Expository Writing Model *Score 3*

San Diego, California, has always been a place where people liked to live. Indians were in the area first. Then Spanish settlers came in 1769. They builded a mission and houses. They liked the harbor. It had deep water so big ships could come in. At first San Diego was a place where people traded cattle skins. They hunted whales and tuna after that. In the twenteth century San Diego was a center for the navy and for making airplanes. San Diego grew from a small town of only 731 people in 1860 to a city of over 1,200,000 people now. They love their city.

Focus/Ideas   Focused on the topic of San Diego's history and development; supported with details including exact dates and figures

Organization/Paragraphs   Good topic sentence; effective use of sequence words and phrases *(first, Then, At first, after that, In the twenteth century)*

Voice   Trustworthy voice but little individuality

Word Choice   Vocabulary often inexact *(place, came, big);* more precise words needed

Sentences   Many short sentences; many sentences beginning with *They*

Conventions   Error in past tense *(builded);* spelling error *(twenteth)*

Expository Writing Model *Score 2*

> Savannah is a very old city in Georgia. It was started in 1733 it was the capital of Georgia. Before Georgia was a state. Savannah is very pretty. They have a nice art museum and lots of good restarons old houses and other buildings. The first steamboat to go across the ochean was called the Savannah and it went from Savannah to england in 1819. People used to go by sailboat before. Savannah has a good climite because it is in the south, it has a population of over 130,000. I have never been in Savannah but I may go.

Focus/Ideas   Concerns topic of Savannah but has no central focus, skipping from fact to fact; unnecessary information about ocean travel

Organization/Paragraphs   Details in no logical order; weak conclusion

Voice   Serious and factual

Word Choice   Inexact vocabulary *(pretty, nice, good)*; overuse of *is, was,* and *go*

Sentences   Little variety; stringy sentences

Conventions   misspellings *(restarons, ochean, climite)*; commas missing from compound sentences and a series; capitalization errors *(england, south)*; fragment and run-on sentences; name of ship to be underlined

Expository Writing Model *Score 1*

London is a very famus old city in england, you always see famus bildings and old things and places there. We went to a museum where they have statews of famus people in wax. I like Britney Spears and Prinses diana. We seen a casel where people have there head choped of. There was a place with Egipchin mummies and a famus stone that people learn to read three langwiches. I didn't the food all the time, there was pizzas and burgers. The buses are red and the taxis are black in London, you have to watch out when you cross the road because people drive on the left and you can hirt.

Focus/Ideas Focused on London with many details; main idea shifts from buildings to food and traffic

Organization/Paragraphs Weak introduction; disorganized body paragraph; lacks conclusion

Voice Writer interested in topic

Word Choice Overuse of *have* and forms of verb *be*

Sentences Most sentences straggly and awkward

Conventions Many misspellings; errors in capitalization *(england, diana)*; no paragraphing; verb tense errors; words missing *(I didn't the food, you can hirt)*; many run-ons

Evaluate Your Writing

You can evaluate your own writing by reading it over carefully. Think about what is good as well as what you can improve. As you read, ask yourself the following questions.

How does my writing sound?   Read it aloud to find out.

- If it sounds choppy, you might combine short sentences.
- Are there many sentences strung together with *and, because,* or *then?* "Unhook" a long stringy sentence by separating it into several sentences.
- Do most sentences begin with *I, the, it, she,* or *he?* Think of other ways to begin these sentences. Simply rearranging words might do the trick.
- Do ideas seem connected? If not, add transition words or phrases such as *finally* or *on the other hand*. These words connect ideas and help your sentences flow.

Is the style appropriate?   Who is your audience? (friends, your principal, a newspaper editor) What is your purpose? (to inform, to persuade, to entertain) Sentence fragments, informal language, and slang may be appropriate for e-mails or quick notes among friends. A more formal style suits written assignments.

Does your writing address the assignment?

- Look for key words in the writing prompt. For example:

  <u>Compare and contrast</u> a <u>bike</u> and a <u>car</u>. Tell <u>two similarities and two differences</u>.

  Topic: bike and car

  What you need to do: Compare and contrast

  What to include: Two similarities and two differences

- Other kinds of key words in writing prompts include *describe, explain, summarize, examples, why,* and *how.*

Is your writing focused?   Are all the sentences about the main idea? Take out or refocus sentences that wander off into unimportant details.

Is there enough elaboration and support?   Your writing may be unclear if you don't elaborate on your ideas. Supply information that readers need to know.

- Use sensory details to make your writing seem fresh and to give readers pictures, but avoid sounding flowery.
- If you give an opinion, supply strong supporting reasons.
- Expand on a main idea with several telling details.
- When necessary, define a term or give examples.

Is your beginning strong?   Does a question, a surprising fact, or an amusing detail capture a reader's interest?

Is your ending satisfying?   A conclusion may restate the main idea in a new way, tell what you feel or what you have learned, or pose a question to readers to think about. Whatever it does, it should signal that you have finished.

Have you used effective words—and not too many of them?   Have you chosen your words carefully?

- Strong verbs, precise nouns, and vivid adjectives make your writing clear and lively.
- Are there awkward phrases you can replace with a word or two? For example, replace *due to the fact that* with *because* and *at this point in time* with *now.*

Check List

- [ ] My writing sounds smooth and easy to read.
- [ ] I have used an appropriate style for my audience and purpose.
- [ ] My writing addresses the prompt or assignment.
- [ ] My writing is focused.
- [ ] I have used enough elaboration and support.
- [ ] I have a strong beginning.
- [ ] I have a satisfying conclusion.
- [ ] I have used effective words and avoided wordiness.

Grammar and Writing Lessons

Declarative and Interrogative Sentences

A **sentence** is a group of words that expresses a complete thought. A sentence begins with a capital letter. A sentence that tells something is a **declarative sentence.** A declarative sentence ends with a period. A sentence that asks a question is an **interrogative sentence.** An interrogative sentence ends with a question mark.

Declarative Sentence	The library is full of interesting books.
Interrogative Sentence	How many of these books have you read?

A Write *D* if the sentence is declarative. Write *I* if the sentence is interrogative.

1. Which region of the country do you like best?

2. The Northeast gets plenty of snow.

3. Is there a state that is always warm?

4. The tallest mountains are in the West.

Write each sentence with the correct end punctuation mark.

5. Last year Al's brother walked the Appalachian Trail

6. How long did it take him

7. He started in May and finished in October

8. Would you go on a hike like that

B Make each word group into a sentence by writing it with correct capitalization and punctuation. Write *D* if the sentence is declarative. Write *I* if the sentence is interrogative.

1. our family is planning a trip to the mountains
2. why are you going in the winter
3. it's fun when the woods are full of snow
4. dad wants to take us all snowshoeing
5. have you ever been on skis
6. is snowboarding as much fun as it looks
7. what would happen if you had an accident
8. we're all going to take skiing lessons
9. do you think you'll go again next year
10. I'd be happy if you would send me a card

C Change each sentence to the kind named in ( ). Write the new sentence.

Example Maria will be home soon. (interrogative)
Will Maria be home soon?

11. Has Maria gone to Florida on vacation? (declarative)
12. Are there alligators in Florida? (declarative)
13. You can swim all year-round in the ocean. (interrogative)
14. Florida oranges do make wonderful juice. (interrogative)
15. Will she call us from the airport? (declarative)

Test Preparation

✓ Write the letter of the word or the word and punctuation mark that complete each sentence.

1. The river is warm in ___

   A Summer   **C** summer

   B summer? **D** summer.

2. ___ fast does it flow?

   A How   **C** How?

   B how   **D** How.

3. Are there many fish in the ___

   A water.   **C** Water

   B water?   **D** water

4. ___ flows into the ocean.

   A It.   **C** It?

   B it   **D** It

✓ Write the letter of the sentence that has correct capitalization and punctuation.

5. **A** Have you visited Arizona?

   B My grandmother retired there

   C she wants us to visit?

   D When are we going.

6. **A** we drove across the country.

   B How did you all fit in the car.

   C It was very crowded.

   D The dog sat on my lap

7. **A** We swam in Lake Superior?

   B It seemed as big as an ocean.

   C Was the water cold.

   D our dog loved it.

8. **A** what did you do then?

   B Did you go to San Francisco.

   C We were out of time.

   D We drove home

Review

✓ Write the mark that should end each sentence. Then write *D* if the sentence is declarative. Write *I* if the sentence is interrogative.

    1. Do you live near the sea

    2. The Atlantic Ocean separates North America from Europe

    3. Can you imagine sailing across the Atlantic

    4. People used to travel by sea for months on end

    5. What did they do all day

✓ Write each sentence. Make any necessary corrections in capitalization and punctuation.

    6. we are studying how people used to travel

    7. my friend Alex is making a model Conestoga wagon

    8. can you imagine what travel was like then

    9. is the Panama Canal in Central America

    10. it is a very important waterway

    11. before the canal, people sailed around South America

    12. were sailing ships very big

    13. Did they take a beating from the waves

    14. the passengers were often sick

    15. how have airplanes made our lives easier

Voice

Voice shows a writer's personality. It reveals feelings and makes one person's writing sound different from everyone else's. A writer's voice gives a piece of writing its tone.

Write the word from the box that describes the voice of each writer.

| funny   serious |

1. Lovell was the smartest dog I ever met. He was a collie that belonged to my uncle Ed. Lovell knew what to do in an emergency. Once he woke up at night and started barking because he smelled smoke. Uncle Ed got his family out of the house quickly. He said that someone might have been hurt if Lovell hadn't barked.

2. Our dog wasn't always called Uh-oh. When we bought him, his name was Rags. As a puppy, though, he was always getting into trouble around the house. He'd eat my sister's shoe or pull down a curtain or make a mess on the floor. Every time he did something wrong, we'd say "Uh-oh!" After a while, the name stuck!

Write three or four sentences about a pet you have known. Use a funny or serious voice.

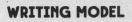

Memoir

A **memoir** tells about an interesting event or experience in your life. It may include information about how you felt, what you saw, or why you did something. Memoirs are also known as personal essays. A memoir that tells a person's life story is called an autobiography.

Introductory paragraph grabs reader's attention.

Details bring scene to life for reader.

Conclusion sums up importance of experience to narrator. Writer reveals feelings.

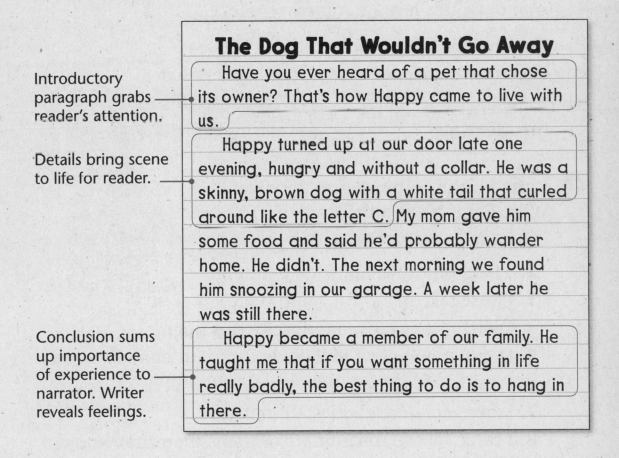

The Dog That Wouldn't Go Away

Have you ever heard of a pet that chose its owner? That's how Happy came to live with us.

Happy turned up at our door late one evening, hungry and without a collar. He was a skinny, brown dog with a white tail that curled around like the letter C. My mom gave him some food and said he'd probably wander home. He didn't. The next morning we found him snoozing in our garage. A week later he was still there.

Happy became a member of our family. He taught me that if you want something in life really badly, the best thing to do is to hang in there.

Imperative and Exclamatory Sentences

An **imperative sentence** gives a command or makes a request. It usually begins with a verb and ends with a period. The subject (*you*) is not shown. An **exclamatory sentence** shows strong feeling or surprise. It ends with an exclamation mark. An **interjection** also shows strong feeling and ends with an exclamation mark. An interjection is a word or group of words, not a complete sentence.

Imperative Sentence	Steer the boat.
Exclamatory Sentence	This river is wide!
	What a trip this is!
Interjection	Amazing! Ouch!

A Write *I* if the sentence is imperative. Write *E* if it is exclamatory.

1. Look at the top of that skyscraper.
2. That's one amazingly tall building!
3. Please take my photograph there.
4. Wow! I've never been in a city this huge!
5. Don't go too close to the edge.
6. Get on any subway train marked 9 or 11.
7. Make sure to read the station names.
8. I can't believe the number of trains there are!
9. What a noise they make!
10. Watch your step when you get off the train.

B Make each word group into a sentence by writing it with correct punctuation. Write *I* if the sentence is imperative. Write *E* if the sentence is exclamatory.

1. Buy your tickets here for the Statue of Liberty
2. What a long line this is
3. Please have your money ready
4. How wonderful the statue looks from the sea
5. Remember to bring your camera
6. Take plenty of pictures
7. Don't miss the bus tour of the city
8. You won't believe how big New York is
9. That bridge is so beautiful
10. Watch your step on the subway

C Add words to change each item below into an interesting sentence. Each item will tell you whether to write an imperative or an exclamatory sentence.

11. the tall Empire State Building (exclamatory)
12. a map of the city (imperative)
13. toys in this store (exclamatory)
14. the busy street (imperative)
15. to the show (imperative)
16. those expensive shoes (exclamatory)
17. the view from the hotel (exclamatory)
18. at the ticket office (imperative)

Test Preparation

Write the letter of the word or the word and punctuation mark that complete each sentence.

1. Notice the bright sunlight and palm trees in ___

  A Florida?

  B Florida.

  C Florida!

  D Florida

2. What a cold, gray place New York is in ___

  A comparison.

  B comparison

  C comparison!

  D comparison?

Write the letter of the imperative or exclamatory sentence that is written correctly.

3. A Cities are incredibly noisy

  B Give me the country any day.

  C Ugh! I couldn't live there?

  D How do you put up with it.

4. A Don't talk to me about the country.

  B I hate mosquitoes?

  C Do you really want to live with cows!

  D I prefer an apartment building

5. A What a wonderful day this is!

  B I could walk in the park forever.

  C Look at all the happy people?

  D Show me a nicer place to be

Review

✓ Write *C* if the end punctuation in the sentence is correct. Write *NC* if the end punctuation is not correct.

1. Tell me how to get to the zoo.
2. Now show me where it is on the map!
3. What a long way off it is.
4. Oops! I'm completely out of money!
5. Please lend me the bus fare.

✓ Write the correct end punctuation for each sentence. Then write *I* if the sentence is imperative and *E* if it is exclamatory.

6. Oh no! We're lost
7. Please help us find our way home
8. Walk to the lights and turn left
9. Catch the A train from platform 4
10. Thank you so much for helping us

✓ Write a word that will make these sentences the kind named in ( ).

11. ___ me the photos you took in Philadelphia. (imperative)
12. ___ an enormous bell that is! (exclamatory)
13. ___ lucky you were it didn't rain! (exclamatory)
14. Please ___ me a copy of that picture. (imperative)
15. ___ my friend Carl on your next visit. (imperative)

Transitions

Transitions are words or phrases that show a relationship between events or ideas. They help the reader by linking sentences or paragraphs. Examples of three common types of transitions are shown below:

Time   first, then, next, before, finally, at last

Place   above, below, beside, here, next to

Comparison and Contrast   however, but, although, on the other hand, like

Choose transition words or phrases from the box to complete the story. Use each word or phrase only once. Capitalize words that begin sentences.

afterward	first	finally	next to
however	at last	opposite	then

Seaman could hardly believe his eyes. **(1)** Hundreds of squirrels were swimming ___ the boat. **(2)** They were crossing to the ___ bank. **(3)** ___, Seaman's master was ignoring him. Seaman barked loudly. **(4)** ___ his master saw the squirrels.

"Go get them, Seaman," he said.

Seaman sprang off the boat into the river. **(5)** ___ he caught a squirrel. **(6)** ___ he brought it back to the boat. **(7)** ___ there was a pile of squirrels on the boat. **(8)** ___ Seaman was quite proud of himself.

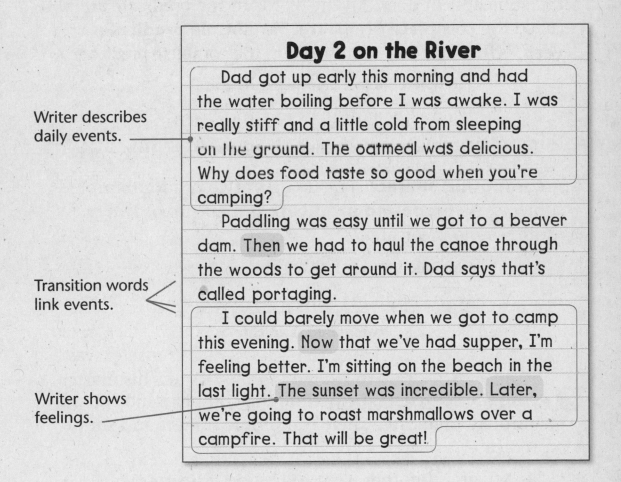

Journal Entry

> A **journal entry** describes your thoughts and experiences during a day in your life. It is part of a journal, recording daily events over a period of weeks, months, or years.

Writer describes daily events.

Transition words link events.

Writer shows feelings.

Day 2 on the River

Dad got up early this morning and had the water boiling before I was awake. I was really stiff and a little cold from sleeping on the ground. The oatmeal was delicious. Why does food taste so good when you're camping?

Paddling was easy until we got to a beaver dam. Then we had to haul the canoe through the woods to get around it. Dad says that's called portaging.

I could barely move when we got to camp this evening. Now that we've had supper, I'm feeling better. I'm sitting on the beach in the last light. The sunset was incredible. Later, we're going to roast marshmallows over a campfire. That will be great!

Subjects and Predicates

The **subject** is the part of the sentence that tells whom or what the sentence is about. All the words in the subject are called the **complete subject**. The **simple subject** is the most important word in the complete subject.

The **predicate** is the part of the sentence that tells what the subject is or does. All the words in the predicate are called the **complete predicate**. The **simple predicate**, or **verb**, is the most important word in the complete predicate.

complete subject complete predicate

My aunt lives in Ohio.

simple subject simple predicate

A **compound subject** is made up of two or more simple subjects. A **compound predicate** is made up of two or more simple predicates.

compound subject

Gina and I live and work in Ohio.

compound predicate

A Write the sentences. Underline the complete subject and complete predicate. Circle the simple subject and simple predicate.

  1. My grandmother went to Ireland last summer.
  2. The village of her ancestors is Portcawl.

B Write each sentence. Draw a line between the complete subject and the complete predicate. Underline the simple subject once and the simple predicate twice.

1. Around 300 million people live in the United States.
2. Some of these residents are recent arrivals.
3. Hong's father came from Vietnam in 1984.
4. He earns a good living in this country.
5. Han's three brothers arrived in San Francisco last year.
6. They work on a farm in Oregon.

C Finish each sentence by adding a complete subject or a complete predicate from the box. Write the sentences.

Complete Subjects
New arrivals in the United States
Many of these immigrants

Complete Predicates
will grow up as Americans
prosper and buy their own businesses

---

(7) ___ often work very hard. **(8)** Some of them ___.
(9) ___ become American citizens after a few years.
(10) Their children ___.

Test Preparation

✔ Write the letter of the phrase that identifies the underlined word or words in each sentence.

1. Jorge and Lourdes <u>are learning English</u>.

   A Simple subject
   B Complete subject
   C Simple predicate
   D Complete predicate

2. The two <u>cousins</u> attend a language school every evening.

   A Simple subject
   B Complete subject
   C Simple predicate
   D Complete predicate

3. <u>Three of their classmates</u> come from Mexico.

   A Simple subject
   B Complete subject
   C Simple predicate
   D Complete predicate

4. Two women <u>are</u> Brazilian.

   A Simple subject
   B Complete subject
   C Simple predicate
   D Complete predicate

5. Other students <u>come from Korea, Japan, and China</u>.

   A Simple subject
   B Complete subject
   C Simple predicate
   D Complete predicate

Review

 Write each sentence. Underline the complete subject once and the complete predicate twice.

1. My friend Michael and I are tutoring English.
2. Two of our classmates meet us every day for half an hour.
3. Dmitri and Olga recently arrived from Russia.
4. They can read and write in English already.
5. Several Russian families have settled in our town.

 Identify the underlined word or words in each sentence. Write *CS* for complete subjects, *CP* for complete predicates, *SS* for simple subjects, or *SP* for simple predicates.

6. <u>The students in our school</u> held an international fair.
7. We <u>served</u> food from all over the world.
8. Several <u>kids</u> dressed in their national costume.
9. Two Japanese girls <u>demonstrated origami</u>.
10. Many <u>families</u> came to visit.

 Look at the letters after each sentence. Write the complete subject when you see *CS*, the simple subject when you see *SS*, the complete predicate when you see *CP*, and the simple predicate when you see *SP.*

11. Three of my teammates are from Mexico.   CS
12. Pedro and Juan play center field and shortstop. CP
13. Jaime is our best pitcher.   SS
14. He won four games so far this year.   SP
15. He pitches again next Saturday.   CP

Sequence

> **Sequence** is the order in which things happen in a story. Transition words such as *before, after, then, next,* and *finally* can tell you when something happens. Days, dates, and times can also help you understand the order of events.

The events in the column below are taken from the paragraph, but they are out of order. Write the events in the correct sequence.

Grandfather left Japan as a young man and went to the United States. Before returning to Japan, he traveled in America. Later, back in the United States, he married and settled in San Francisco. There he had a daughter. After many years, he took his family back to Japan.

settled in San Francisco

got married

returned to Japan as young man

left Japan as young man

traveled throughout America

had daughter

took family to Japan

Write about a trip. Tell four things you did in order. Use transition words.

Postcard

A **postcard** is a brief message, with a picture on one side, sent by mail to friends or family. Often a postcard gives details about a place you are visiting on vacation and describes your feelings about being there.

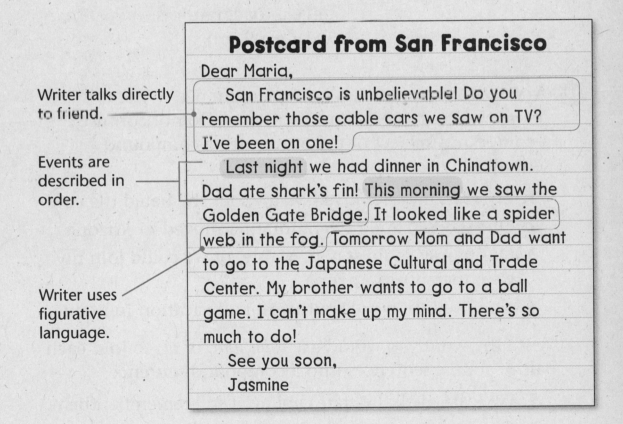

Postcard from San Francisco

Dear Maria,

San Francisco is unbelievable! Do you remember those cable cars we saw on TV? I've been on one!

Last night we had dinner in Chinatown. Dad ate shark's fin! This morning we saw the Golden Gate Bridge. It looked like a spider web in the fog. Tomorrow Mom and Dad want to go to the Japanese Cultural and Trade Center. My brother wants to go to a ball game. I can't make up my mind. There's so much to do!

See you soon,
Jasmine

Writer talks directly to friend.

Events are described in order.

Writer uses figurative language.

Compound Sentences

> A **compound sentence** is made up of two simple sentences joined by a comma and a connecting word such as *and, but,* or *or.*
>
> | **Simple Sentences** | The horned toad looks like a toad. |
> |---|---|
> | | It is really a lizard. |
> | **Compound Sentence** | The horned toad looks like a toad, but it is really a lizard. |

A Write *S* if the sentence is a simple sentence. Write *C* if the sentence is a compound sentence. Do not confuse a compound subject or predicate with a compound sentence.

1. My grandmother loved Maine, but she hated the cold.
2. One day she and my grandfather moved to Arizona.
3. Our family could stay in Maine, or we could join my grandparents in Arizona.
4. Now we live in the Southwest and vacation in Maine.

Write the word you would use (*and, but,* or *or*) to join each pair of simple sentences into a compound sentence.

5. We learned all the state capitals. I still remember them.
6. New York is a huge city. It is not the state capital.

B Join each pair of simple sentences to make a compound sentence. Use the word *and, but,* or *or.* Capitalize the new sentence correctly. Do not forget to add a comma.

1. My uncle bought some land in Utah.
   He is building a cabin on it.

2. According to my dad, it's a silly idea.
   My uncle disagrees.

3. My uncle has tall trees on his land.
   They will provide the wood.

4. My uncle called me last week. He asked for my help.

5. I could go to camp this summer. I could help my uncle.

6. Camp is fun. It might be more fun to build a cabin.

C Form compound sentences by adding a sentence in the box to each numbered item below. Use the word *and, but,* or *or.* Do not forget to capitalize correctly and to add a comma.

I might study forestry.

I'm not feeling tired.

Mom will take us on a hike there.

They don't bother people.

---

7. We walked a long way today ___

8. I might become a park ranger one day ___

9. There are bears in these woods ___

10. We are going to the state park next weekend ___

Test Preparation

✓ Write the letter of the word or the word and punctuation mark that complete each sentence.

1. Grandpa told stories at night ____ we stayed up to listen.

   A , and   **C** , or

   B and,   **D** and

2. In one story he had scared a ghost ____ in another he had tamed a tornado.

   A and   **C** or

   B , and   **D** or,

3. Once a rattlesnake tried to bite Gramps ____ he bit the snake instead.

   A , or   **C** , but

   B and   **D** and,

4. According to Mom these were crazy stories ____ we loved them.

   A or,   **C** but,

   B and   **D** , but

5. Sometimes our friends would visit ____ they'd listen too.

   A , and   **C** and

   B , or   **D** but,

6. Do you want to hear about the grizzly ____ do you want the story about the alligator?

   A , but   **C** or,

   B , or   **D** and,

7. Once Grandpa was swimming ____ a big catfish swallowed him whole.

   A , but   **C** , and

   B , or   **D** but,

Review

✓ Write *S* if the sentence is a simple sentence. If it is a compound sentence, write it with a comma in the correct place.

1. Some stories are true but others are not.
2. Was Paul Bunyan a real person or was he fictitious?
3. I think giants may exist but a blue ox is unbelievable!
4. Ms. Armstrong first told the story and then read it to us.
5. I like both made-up stories and true stories.

✓ Use the conjunction *and, but,* or *or* to join each pair of sentences. Write the new sentences. Remember to capitalize correctly and to add a comma.

6. We are reading a new book in class. It's really interesting.
7. At first I didn't like it. Now I can't wait for the next story.
8. The first story was a tall tale. The second one was a myth.
9. Tall tales can be violent. Usually they are funny.
10. The myths are strange. Some of them are scary.
11. They are like fairy tales. There are no knights or dragons.
12. Our group chose a story. We'll present it to the class.
13. We could make a cartoon of our story. We could act it out.
14. Costumes would be fun. None of us can sew.

Know Your Purpose

Authors write for different reasons, or **purposes.** They might want to inform, persuade, or entertain their readers. They might want to express their feelings or create a mood. Whatever reason an author has for writing, his or her purpose should be clear.

 Each numbered item describes the topic of a piece of writing. Write the letter of the purpose that best suits each topic.

> **A** To entertain   **B** To inform   **C** To persuade

1. Why James Lopez should be president

2. The difference between tornadoes and hurricanes

3. A recipe for brownies

4. The day my hamster stole my lunch

5. What this school needs most

6. The funniest story I ever heard

7. Dogs should be kept on leashes

8. How to write a research paper

Write two or three sentences about a pet. Write with the purpose of informing, persuading, or entertaining your reader.

E-mail Invitation

An **e-mail invitation** is a quick way to let friends know about an event. Like an invitation sent by regular mail, an e-mail invitation tells when and where the event is taking place, along with any other useful information. Unlike a regular invitation, it travels instantly, via the Internet.

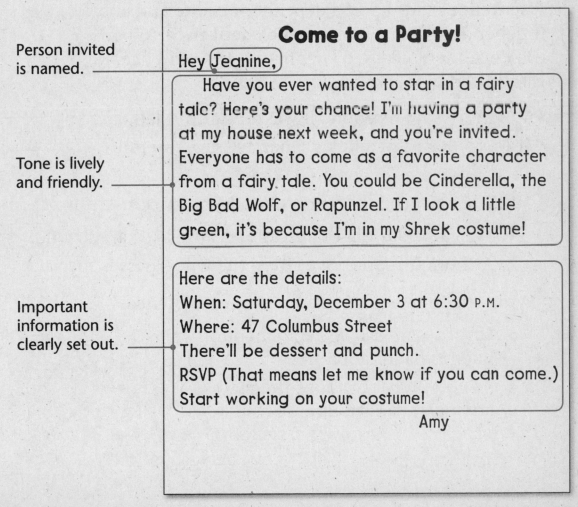

Person invited is named.

Come to a Party!

Hey Jeanine,

Have you ever wanted to star in a fairy tale? Here's your chance! I'm having a party at my house next week, and you're invited. Everyone has to come as a favorite character from a fairy tale. You could be Cinderella, the Big Bad Wolf, or Rapunzel. If I look a little green, it's because I'm in my Shrek costume!

Tone is lively and friendly.

Important information is clearly set out.

Here are the details:
When: Saturday, December 3 at 6:30 P.M.
Where: 47 Columbus Street
There'll be dessert and punch.
RSVP (That means let me know if you can come.)
Start working on your costume!

Amy

Clauses and Complex Sentences

A clause is a group of words with a subject and a verb. A **dependent clause** begins with a word such as *because* or *when*. It cannot stand alone as a sentence. An **independent clause** can stand alone.

Dependent Clause   when we saw Yosemite
Independent Clause It was a beautiful fall day.

A sentence made up of a dependent clause and an independent clause is a **complex sentence.** When the dependent clause comes first in the sentence, it is followed by a comma.

• When we saw Yosemite, it was a beautiful fall day.
• It was a beautiful fall day when we saw Yosemite.

A Write the dependent clause in each sentence.

1. We value our national parks because they are so wild.

2. Although people love cities, the wilderness is special.

Write the independent clause in each sentence.

3. Until a law was passed, our country had no national parks.

4. As you probably know, there are many parks today.

B Write the clause in the sentence that is named in ( ).
I stands for *independent* and *D* for *dependent.*

1. Since I last wrote, we've made big plans. (I)
2. After school gets out, Ted can take us camping. (D)
3. We'll go to Baxter State Park because it's really wild. (I)
4. If the weather is good, we can climb Mt. Katahdin. (D)
5. We won't plan our route until we've studied the map. (D)
6. Before we go, we need to decide about food. (D)
7. Although the trip is just a week, we'll need many items. (I)
8. It will be hard work because we'll have heavy packs. (D)
9. Ted won't take us on the trip unless we follow his orders. (I)
10. Let me know soon if you can come. (I)

C Combine each pair of simple sentences. Use the word in ( ). Write the complex sentence.

11. The weather was beautiful. We got to the park. (when)
12. We couldn't see the mountain. It was dark. (because)
13. We lit a fire. We found a campsite. (after)
14. Even burned oatmeal tastes good! You are hungry. (if)
15. We'll have a good breakfast. We leave tomorrow. (before)

Test Preparation

☑ Write the letter of the independent clause in each group.

1. **A** unless you want to freeze

    B when you pack

    C if you like hot food

    D carry matches with you

2. **A** because we started late

    B although we're very tired

    C we have a long way to go

    D since we got lost

3. **A** I look forward to lunch

    B after we've walked a long way

    C when I'm camping

    D because I get really hungry

4. **A** after we get home

    B unless they're really bad

    C I'll send you some photos

    D if you're interested

☑ Write the letter of the word that should introduce each dependent clause.

5. ___ we can't light a fire, we'll eat sandwiches.

    A Or   **C** Before

    B Since   **D** But

6. The dog growls ___ she hears the coyotes howling.

    A although   **C** or

    B when   **D** but

7. I'm going to need a rest ___ we get to the summit.

    A since   **C** and

    B because   **D** after

8. ___ there's a tornado, we're going to make it!

    A Until   **C** When

    B Since   **D** Unless

Review

☑ Write *I* if the underlined group of words is an independent clause. Write *D* if it is a dependent clause.

1. When school is out, <u>we will visit my uncle Bill</u>.
2. <u>Before he retired</u>, he worked in New York City.
3. He moved to Vermont <u>after he bought an old farm</u>.
4. Although he's not a farmer, <u>he loves life in Vermont</u>.
5. <u>We will stay all of August</u> unless the weather's bad.
6. <u>If there are mosquitoes</u>, my mom will want to go home.
7. <u>It's fun for me</u> because Uncle Bill has a pond.
8. Once we went swimming <u>as the full moon was rising</u>.
9. Since my sister's only three, <u>she can't swim yet</u>.
10. I hope we can stay <u>until school begins</u>.

☑ Combine each pair of simple sentences. Use the word in ( ). Write the complex sentence.

11. Lou sat in the front. He had never been in a canoe. (since)
12. We paddled upstream. We were tired. (until)
13. We stopped. We came to a good place for lunch. (when)
14. The swimming was great. The water was cold. (although)
15. We'll go as far as Lake Banyan. It begins to rain. (unless)
16. Canoe trips are fun. The weather is good. (if)

Style

Too many short, simple sentences can make your writing dull and choppy. Create a smooth, flowing **style** by combining simple sentences to create compound or complex sentences.

Simple Sentences	We were tired. We wanted to reach the summit.
Compound Sentence	We were tired, but we wanted to reach the summit.
Complex Sentence	Although we were tired, we wanted to reach the summit.

 Combine the two short, choppy sentences. Use the word in ( ). Write the compound or complex sentence.

1. It was three in the afternoon. We finally reached the summit. (when)

2. We were all hungry. We stopped for lunch. (and)

 Write a short narrative about a place that you love to visit. Include at least one compound sentence and one complex sentence.

Writing for Tests

Prompt Think about a time when you took <u>a trip</u>—maybe for a vacation or a family visit. What <u>experience</u> stays in your mind? Write a <u>narrative</u> describing this event to a <u>friend or family member</u>.

Compound and complex sentences create a flowing style.

Author uses vivid words and images to recall interesting incidents.

Sentences vary in style and length.

Flying Solo

When I was six years old, I flew to New York City alone! I had been on an airplane only once before, and I was hopping up and down with excitement. A hostess held my hand as I waved goodbye to my mom and dad. She took me onto the plane and helped me fix the seat belt.

The plane roared when it took off. I tried to squeeze my armrest, but I grabbed the lady sitting next to me instead. She screamed! Later I spilled orange juice on her dress. I loved making my seat go backwards and forwards. After I did this for a while, the lady next to me found another place to sit.

My aunt met me at the airport. I stayed with her for two weeks, but I remember that flight best of all.

Common and Proper Nouns

- A noun is a word that names a person, place, or thing.
- A **common noun** names any person, place, or thing.
- A **proper noun** names a particular person, place, or thing. Proper nouns begin with capital letters.

Common Nouns   The <u>game</u> will be next <u>week</u>.

Proper Nouns   <u>Amy</u> will play <u>Saturday</u>.

Some proper nouns have more than one word, such as *Boston Red Sox*. Some include titles that tell what a person is or does, such as *Ms. Gomez* or *Professor Chu*.

A One of the underlined words or word groups in each sentence is a noun. Write that noun. Then write *C* if it is a common noun and *P* if it is a proper noun.

1. <u>Our</u> local soccer <u>team</u> is the Comets.
2. The Comets <u>play</u> their home <u>games</u> in Burgess Field.
3. <u>Julio Lopez</u> led the team in scoring <u>last</u> year.
4. He <u>will</u> play in the all-star game next <u>month</u>.
5. The <u>Comets</u> don't have as <u>many</u> fans as our team.
6. I'm getting my <u>friends</u> to go to soccer games <u>with</u> me.
7. They <u>like</u> the atmosphere at <u>Burgess Field</u>.
8. The food is good, and <u>tickets</u> are <u>cheap</u>.

B Write the three nouns in each sentence. Write *C* if a noun is a common noun. Write *P* if a noun is a proper noun.

1. Do you enjoy football, basketball, or hockey best?
2. In New England my favorite team is the Patriots.
3. My family attended a game last December.
4. Snow was falling, and a cold wind was blowing that Sunday.
5. We saw our neighbor, Mr. Liano, in his heaviest coat.
6. Mrs. Liano had her scarf wrapped around her face.
7. The players were slipping on patches of icy mud.
8. Our hands were freezing, but we had food and hot drinks.
9. Coach Belichick looked cold in his sweatshirt and gloves.
10. Finally, the Eagles were beaten, and the crowd left the stadium.
11. It was a long drive back to Boston that night.
12. I will buy tickets for outdoor events only in July!

C Write common or proper nouns of your own choice to complete the paragraph. Write *C* for common nouns and *P* for proper nouns.

   (13) The big game is next ___ at seven o'clock. **(14)** ___ says that his team is ready to play. **(15)** All the players are healthy and eager to meet their rivals from ___.
(16) There'll be a party after the game in the school ___.
(17) My mom's ___ is broken, so I can't offer you a ride.
(18) Maybe you can get a ride with ___.

Test Preparation

 Write the letter of the word or words that are a common noun.

1. Did you watch the Nuggets in the playoff game last year?

    A watch   **C** game

    B Nuggets   **D** last

2. I don't follow soccer, but this game was exciting.

    A follow   **C** this

    B soccer   **D** but

3. Everyone in Springfield went wild at the final whistle.

    A Springfield **C** final

    B wild   **D** whistle

4. They drove their cars up and down Main Street all night.

    A cars   **C** Main Street

    B down   **D** all

 Write the letter of the word or words that are a proper noun.

5. The Ice Bears is the name of our hockey team.

    A Ice Bears **C** hockey

    B name   **D** team

6. Practices are every Tuesday and Thursday at 7 o'clock.

    A Practices **C** Thursday

    B every   **D** o'clock

7. The team plays all its games at the Tey Arena.

    A team   **C** games

    B plays   **D** Tey Arena

8. That's the big green building on Elm Avenue.

    A That's   **C** building

    B green   **D** Elm Avenue

Review

✓ Two nouns are underlined in each sentence. Write the common noun if (C) follows the sentence. Write the proper noun if (P) follows the sentence.

1. My brother Carlos plays <u>baseball</u> for <u>Lincoln High</u>. (C)
2. Next <u>Tuesday</u> he's pitching in a big <u>game</u>. (P)
3. This is a <u>playoff</u> against the <u>Marauders</u>. (P)
4. Carlos's <u>team</u> is the <u>Leopards</u>. (P)
5. The Leopards have one <u>loss</u>—to the Marauders last <u>September</u>. (C)
6. The <u>winner</u> will be champs of the <u>Eastern Division</u>. (P)
7. The <u>game</u> will be played at <u>Rugby College</u>. (C)
8. The winning team plays in the state <u>final</u> in <u>June</u>. (C)
9. <u>Mr. Morrison</u> is taking me to the <u>stadium</u>. (P)
10. We'll catch the <u>train</u> from <u>Washington Street</u>. (C)
11. <u>Carlos</u> is such a good <u>pitcher</u>. (P)
12. One <u>day</u> I bet he'll pitch for the <u>Atlanta Braves</u>. (C)

✓ Write the three nouns in each sentence. Write *C* if a noun is a common noun. Write *P* if a noun is a proper noun.

13. The Red Sox hadn't won a championship in 86 years.
14. Then the team faced New York in the playoffs.
15. The series lasted for seven games, and the Sox won!
16. Next they beat the Cardinals from St. Louis in the World Series.

Figurative Language

> Good writers sometimes use **figurative language** to present ideas in fresh, new ways. Here are some types of figurative language.
>
> - A **simile** uses the word *like* or *as* to compare two unlike things.
>
>   That player is tall as a tree.
>
> - A **metaphor** compares two unlike things without using *like* or *as*.
>
>   The game was a war from beginning to end.
>
> - **Personification** gives an animal, object, or idea human characteristics.
>
>   The sun smiled on us when we left the gym.
>
> - **Hyperbole** is a form of exaggeration used to make a point.
>
>   I could have slept for a year after that game.

Identify the figure of speech in each sentence.

1. The basket was a mile away.
2. I charged down the court like an angry bull.
3. The ball jumped into my hands.
4. Suddenly I was an eagle.
5. The ball had eyes and saw exactly where to go.
6. That was the game of the century.

Write several sentences describing a summer day at the pool or beach. Use at least two figures of speech.

Poem

A **poem** is like a salad: it can include many ingredients. Almost all poems are written in lines— or verse—and use interesting, imaginative language. Many poems also use catchy rhymes and rhythms.

Slam Dunk

Lines are grouped to form stanzas.

> I'm a bird
> (that's the word)
> when I call
> for the ball.

Words and lines are spaced to aid meaning.

> I   have   space.
>
> I'm   all   grace.

End words rhyme.

> Look up there
> in the air!

Poet uses figurative, imaginative language and format.

> W i n g s s p r e a d
> above your head,
> I swoop
> for the hoop
> like a hawk
> for a fish.

> Swish!

Regular Plural Nouns

- Singular nouns name one person, place, or thing. **Plural nouns** name more than one person, place, or thing.

- Add -*s* to form the plural of most nouns.

  school/schools   dog/dogs   cow/cows

- Add -*es* to form plurals of nouns that end in *ch, sh, s, ss,* or *x.*

  ranch/ranches   bush/bushes   gas/gases

  cross/crosses   fox/foxes

- To form the plural of nouns that end in a consonant followed by a *y,* change the *y* to *i* and add -*es.*

  family/families   party/parties   pony/ponies

A Write the plural noun in each sentence.

1. The students at my mom's school all dressed the same.
2. They wore blue and white uniforms.
3. They ate their lunches outside when the weather was nice.
4. Once Mom threw her food into the bushes!
5. She says her teachers were good.
6. Classes were small, and the work was interesting.
7. There weren't many after-school activities.
8. The only teams were basketball and softball.

B Write the plural form of the noun in ( ) in each sentence.

1. Last summer our family visited my uncles' (ranch).
2. Some (day) the men would cut down trees.
3. My (brother) and I wanted to cut trees too.
4. We found a tall pine far from the (house).
5. We didn't have saws, so we all grabbed (ax).
6. The tree came down with loud (crash).
7. It missed me by (inch)!
8. We never told the (family), but we learned our lesson.
9. We didn't want them to make (fuss).
10. Our (sister) still laugh at us, but it's really not funny.
11. At least we didn't cry like (baby).
12. However, we will stick to trimming (bush).

C Complete the paragraph with plural forms of nouns in the box. Write the paragraph. Use each noun only once.

box	dish	bench
carton	lady	sandwich

(13) At school we eat lunch sitting on ___ in the cafeteria. (14) Mom packs my ___ in a brown paper bag. (15) Some kids bring colorful plastic ___. (16) We drink our milk out of cardboard ___. (17) The ___ in charge make us throw our waste paper away. (18) There are no ___ or silverware to wash.

Test Preparation

 Write the letter of the correct plural form that completes each sentence.

1. My dad has had several ___.

   A jobz   **C** jobs

   B jobes   **D** jobies

2. He has sold ___ in a department store.

   A watchs   **C** watch's

   B watches   **D** watchies

3. Once he worked as a clown for children's ___.

   A partys   **C** partyses

   B partyies   **D** parties

4. Whatever the job, he has had to pay ___!

   A taxes   **C** taxies

   B taxs   **D** taxs'

 Write the letter of the ending that will form the plural of the singular noun in each phrase.

5. driving truck

   A -es   **C** -ies

   B -'s   **D** -s

6. riding donkey

   A -s   **C** -ies

   B -sies   **D** -es

7. making dress

   A -is   **C** -es

   B -ies   **D** -'s

8. selling brush

   A -is   **C** -ez

   B -es   **D** -'s

Review

✓ Write the two plural nouns in each sentence.

1. Most evenings my sister Shana and I do our homework in our rooms.
2. One night, bright flashes suddenly lit up the skies.
3. Loud crashes of thunder seemed to shake the walls of the house.
4. Shana and I peered through our bedroom windows across the dark valleys.
5. Lightning had struck the steeples of several tall churches in the area.

✓ Write the plural forms of the nouns in ( ) in each sentence.

6. Name some (thing) that you learned in your (class) today.
7. Well, in science class I learned the (name) of three common (gas).
8. And did you know that (caterpillar) become (butterfly)?
9. We studied (type) of (grass) that grow on the prairie.
10. The teacher told us that (monkey) use their (tail) like an extra hand.
11. In social studies I learned that our (tax) help pay for our (school).
12. We read (story) about a boy and a girl who were given three (wish).

Include Necessary Information

Writers of news stories must be careful to **include necessary information** in their reports. The basic rule for a news reporter is to answer the questions *who, what, where, when,* and *why* when telling about an event.

Each group of sentences gives information about an event. Write whether the information answers the question *who, what, where, when,* or *why.*

1. Information for an article in the school newspaper:
   A There was an assembly.
   B It took place at 1 P.M. on Friday, December 12.
   C The assembly was about winning a poetry contest.
   D The assembly took place in the school auditorium.
   E Students in grades 3–5 attended.

2. Information for an article in a community newspaper:
   A A softball game was played.
   B Jefferson School played Copernicus School.
   C The game was on June 8 at 3 P.M.
   D The game was to decide the softball championship.
   E The game was played at Emerson Field.

Write a short news story about a real or imaginary event at your school. Include all necessary information.

News Story

A **news story** gives readers information about recent events, from around the world to around your school. Whatever the subject, news stories focus on the facts. They answer the questions *who, what, where, when,* and *why*—known as the 5 Ws. They may also answer the question *how*. Writers of news stories should never give their opinions.

Necessary information is in first paragraph.

Less important details come later in story.

Quotations add interest to story.

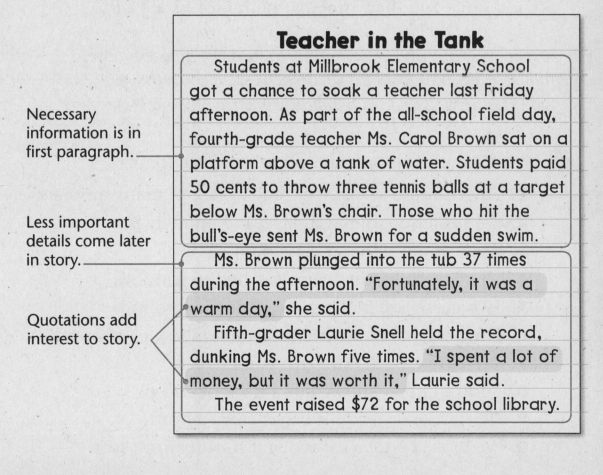

Teacher in the Tank

Students at Millbrook Elementary School got a chance to soak a teacher last Friday afternoon. As part of the all-school field day, fourth-grade teacher Ms. Carol Brown sat on a platform above a tank of water. Students paid 50 cents to throw three tennis balls at a target below Ms. Brown's chair. Those who hit the bull's-eye sent Ms. Brown for a sudden swim.

Ms. Brown plunged into the tub 37 times during the afternoon. "Fortunately, it was a warm day," she said.

Fifth-grader Laurie Snell held the record, dunking Ms. Brown five times. "I spent a lot of money, but it was worth it," Laurie said.

The event raised $72 for the school library.

Irregular Plural Nouns

A plural noun names more than one person, place, or thing. Many nouns add -*s* to form the plural. An **irregular plural noun** has a special form for the plural.

Singular Nouns	The <u>child</u> kept a pet <u>mouse</u>.
Irregular Plural Nouns	The <u>children</u> kept pet <u>mice</u>.

Some nouns and their irregular plural forms are *calf/ calves, child/children, deer/deer, foot/feet, goose/geese, leaf/leaves, life/lives, loaf/loaves, man/men, moose/moose, mouse/mice, sheep/sheep, shelf/shelves, tooth/teeth, wife/ wives, wolf/wolves,* and *woman/women.*

A Write the irregular plural noun in each sentence.

1. The children at our school take care of many animals.
2. We make sure our animals lead happy lives.
3. We keep mice in our classroom.
4. The fish tanks are on shelves by the window.
5. Two geese live in a pen near the playground.
6. They eat grain and crumbs from old loaves of bread.
7. Once we looked after two young deer.
8. A local farmer showed us a flock of sheep.
9. He also let us feed his calves from a bottle.
10. We looked after a cat when it hurt its front feet.

B Write the plural form of each underlined singular noun.

1. In school we are studying the <u>life</u> of frontier <u>family</u>.
2. <u>Man</u> had to do many difficult <u>task</u> every day.
3. Their <u>wife</u> worked hard in their homes and <u>garden</u>.
4. Even the <u>cat</u> had to work at catching <u>mouse</u>!
5. The <u>child</u> also had to help with family <u>chore</u>.
6. They might feed the hens, <u>duck</u>, and <u>goose</u>.
7. In the fall <u>boy</u> and girls would help rake <u>leaf</u> into piles and burn them.
8. Men would hunt and bring home <u>deer</u> or <u>moose</u>.
9. Sometimes <u>wolf</u> would steal <u>sheep</u> from the pasture.
10. Men, <u>woman</u>, and children had to work very hard in those <u>day</u>.

C Complete the sentences with plural forms of nouns in the box. Write the sentences.

child	foot	loaf	tooth	wolf

11. Every Friday afternoon in winter, my grandmother bakes ___ of crusty raisin bread.
12. I rush home from school on Friday as fast as my ___ will carry me.
13. Sometimes Grandma will invite other ___ from the neighborhood to come to our house.
14. We attack the hot bread like hungry ___.
15. We just can't wait to get our ___ into that fresh raisin bread.

Test Preparation

✓ Write the letter of the correct plural form for each underlined word.

1. <u>Goose</u> walk on big yellow flip-flops!

   A Goose   **C** Geese

   B Gooses   **D** Geeses

2. <u>Wolf</u> have soft and furry paws.

   A Wolves   **C** Wolfes

   B Wolvs   **D** Wolvies

3. What are your <u>foot</u> like?

   A feets   **C** foots

   B feet   **D** feete

4. The ones that <u>mouse</u> have are very tiny.

   A mouses   **C** moose

   B mices   **D** mice

5. <u>Moose</u> have hard hooves.

   A Mooses   **C** Moose

   B Mouses   **D** Mice

6. So do <u>sheep</u>.

   A sheeps   **C** sheep

   B sheepses   **D** sheepies

Review

☑ Write the word in ( ) that completes each sentence.

1. Last fall the Murray brothers boasted that they would find two (mooses, moose).
2. They tramped noisily over twigs and (leaves, leafs).
3. An angry bull moose charged the two (men, mens).
4. The brothers dropped their gear and ran like (deer, deeres).

☑ Write the plural form of each underlined singular noun.

5. Meanwhile, the <u>wife</u> of the Murray brothers decided that they would go hunting.
6. They broke up two <u>loaf</u> of bread.
7. A flock of <u>goose</u> flew down to eat the crumbs.
8. One of the <u>woman</u> caught a fat goose in a net.

☑ Complete the paragraph with plural forms of nouns in the box. Write the words.

foot	life	mouse	shelf	tooth

(9) I have two white ___ named Georgette and Zelda. (10) They live in a wire cage on one of the ___ in my bedroom. (11) Georgette loves to climb up the sides and cling with her tiny ___. (12) Zelda prefers to clean her yellow ___ by chewing on a piece of wood. (13) Georgette and Zelda lead active ___.

Visual Details

Good writing helps the reader "see" what is happening. Writers provide **visual details** with exact and vivid nouns, adjectives, verbs, and figures of speech.

Weak A dinosaur came quickly toward us out of the forest.

Strong A tyrannosaurus burst from a tangle of creepers and lunged at us.

Read the paragraph. Then find items in the box that give stronger visual details than the underlined words. Rewrite the paragraph using words from the box.

blue-green glow	wriggled	monstrous
a ghastly mask of terror	slimy	dash

(1) The <u>wet</u> creature crawled across the field toward the houses. (2) Its body gave off a <u>light</u>. (3) When it <u>moved</u> over the grass, it left a sticky trail. (4) Two or three people who had not found shelter tried to <u>run</u> to the forest. (5) One man's face was <u>scared</u> as he stumbled. (6) The <u>big</u> shape had terrified the entire village.

Think of two or three characters for a television show or play. Write strong visual details to describe them.

Play Scene/Skit

> A **play scene** or **skit** is a brief story told in dialogue—the words that the characters actually say. A play is meant to be performed before an audience, but a reader can imagine what is happening by reading the lines and the author's descriptions of the action. The descriptions of action are known as the stage directions.

Characters are listed at the beginning.

Dialogue is lively and realistic.

Stage directions give visual details.

Real Life

Characters

SAM   EDY, Sam's sister

Sam's bedroom. Sam and Edy are in front of the television, operating video game controls. The room's one window is behind them.

SAM: This is so awesome. Look at that thing.

EDY: Watch out! It's trying to get you! Zap it!

SAM *(working frantically)*: Gotcha!

(The window fills with a greenish light.)

SAM: Oh, man! Here's another one!

EDY: Let me get this one. Come on, boy.

(A long, green tentacle slowly enters the room through the window.)

SAM *(his eyes fixed on the screen)*: Nice one!

EDY *(giving Sam a high five)*: Ha! So long, space aliens.

(The tentacle withdraws. The light fades.)

Singular Possessive Nouns

A **possessive noun** shows ownership. A **singular possessive noun** shows that one person, place, or thing has or owns something. Add an apostrophe (') and the letter s to a singular noun to make it possessive.

Singular Nouns	<u>Jim</u> had a job in a store owned by his <u>uncle</u>.
Singular Possessive Nouns	<u>Jim's</u> job was in his <u>uncle's</u> store.

A Write the singular possessive noun in ( ) that completes each sentence.

1. My (brother, brother's) first job was at a car wash.
2. He had to polish each (customer, customer's) car.
3. Once he forgot to clean a (woman's, womans') windshield.
4. The boss fined my brother a (days, day's) pay.
5. The (car's, cares) owner said that this wasn't fair.
6. She offered Jim work at her (husbands', husband's) pizzeria.
7. (Jim's, Jims) new job was to make tomato sauce for pizza.
8. He also had to take each (diners', diner's) order.

B Write the possessive form of each underlined singular noun.

1. A <u>doctor</u> education takes many years of schooling.
2. A <u>nurse</u> training is shorter.
3. My dad says that a <u>carpenter</u> life is interesting.
4. He enjoys a <u>lumberyard</u> sounds and smells.
5. My <u>sister</u> goal is to become a teacher.
6. She says that an <u>educator</u> job is never dull.
7. Our <u>teacher</u> name is Ms. Bond.
8. I asked for <u>Ms. Bond</u> opinion about teaching.
9. She told me about her <u>job</u> pros and cons.
10. I want to learn more about our <u>principal</u> work too.
11. <u>Mr. Cruz</u> job must be hard sometimes.
12. He knows every <u>student</u> name and record.

C Write a singular possessive noun to complete each sentence.

13. A(n) ____ place of work is a theater.
14. If you like food, a(n) ____ job might interest you.
15. A(n) ____ life involves a great deal of traveling.
16. You need a college education for a(n) ____ career.
17. A(n) ____ job would be good for you if you like working outdoors.
18. When our dog was sick, we took her to the ____ office.
19. When our car needs a tune-up, we take it to the ____ garage.
20. You need good writing skills for a(n) ____ job.

Test Preparation

Write the letter of the singular possessive noun that completes each sentence.

1. My ___ instructions were very clear.

   A boss's   C bosses'
   B bosses   D boss

2. Sand this ___ surface until it is smooth.

   A tables   C tables'
   B table's   D tables's

3. That should be no more than an ___ work.

   A hour   C hours'
   B hours   D hour's

4. Next, go to ___ office and help her.

   A Mrs. Kona   C Mrs. Kona's
   B Mrs. Konas   D Mrs. Konas'

5. Don't trip over the ___ dish on the way.

   A dogs's   C dog's
   B dogs   D dogs'

6. Use a file to sharpen this ___ blade.

   A saw's   C saw'z
   B saws   D saws'

7. When the phone rings, take each ___ request.

   A caller   C caller'es
   B callers   D caller's

8. Enter every order in the ___ database.

   A computers'   C computers
   B computer's   D computers's

Review

✓ Write the possessive form of each underlined noun.

1. a <u>doctor</u> stethoscope
2. a <u>salesclerk</u> register
3. <u>Mr. Dunn</u> 18-wheeler
4. a <u>sailor</u> uniform
5. a <u>farmer</u> tractor

✓ If the underlined word is written correctly, write *C*. If it is incorrect, write it correctly.

6. Let's make a bookshelf for <u>Maria's</u> birthday present.
7. It shouldn't take more than a <u>mornings</u> work.
8. We can use <u>Dads'</u> tool kit.
9. What is an average <u>books's</u> height?
10. This <u>screwdrivers</u> head is too big for these screws.

✓ Complete the paragraph with singular possessive forms of nouns in the box. Write the words.

clock	mom	night	school	vacation

(11) I had a wonderful ___ sleep. (12) For once, my ___ noisy alarm didn't go off. (13) I finally woke up to the smell of my ___ famous pancakes. (14) It was great to realize that our ___ doors were closed until September. (15) Summer ___ first days are always the best!

Time-Order Words

Writers use **time-order words** to describe the order in which to do something or to tell readers exactly when events took place. Words and phrases such as *first, then, after that,* and *finally* can make a process clear and a story understandable.

Confusing	Use a ladle to drop mixed-up milk, flour, and eggs into a hot pan.
Clear	<u>First</u>, heat the pan. <u>Next</u>, mix milk, flour, and eggs. <u>Finally</u>, ladle the mixture into the pan.

Write the time-order word or phrase in each sentence.

1. Marven woke the lumberjacks before dawn.
2. He always woke up Pierre last.
3. After that, Marven had his breakfast.
4. He then spent the morning working with Mr. Murray.
5. After dinner, Marven might write a letter to his family.

Rewrite the instructions in the correct order, using time-order words or phrases. Add your own concluding sentence.

Call people to breakfast.
Clear the table and wash the dishes.
Set the table and prepare the pancakes.
Serve everyone pancakes.

Describe a Job

A **job description** tells the person who is going to do the job exactly what to do. Because it includes important information, a job description must be well-organized and clearly written.

Each paragraph describes a separate task.

Taking Care of Fifi

Give Fifi breakfast no later than 8 A.M. She gets one scoop of dry cereal and two spoonfuls from a can in the refrigerator. Put her in the backyard for a few minutes after breakfast.

Writer includes important details.

At midday, Fifi needs a good walk. Her leash is hanging up in the hall. Don't take her to the park because the other dogs frighten her.

Time-order words and phrases make instructions clear.

Come back again at six to give Fifi her supper. She gets two scoops of dry cereal. Then take her out for another walk.

Finally, put Fifi to bed. Remember that she likes to sleep with the chewy rubber rabbit. Say good night to her and tell her I'll be back soon.

LESSON 10

Plural Possessive Nouns

A **plural possessive noun** shows that something is owned or shared by more than one person, place, or thing.

- Add an apostrophe (') to plural nouns ending in *-s, -es,* or *-ies.*

  our <u>Presidents'</u> pets   the <u>countries'</u> leaders

- Add an apostrophe (') and *-s* to a plural noun that does not end in *-s, -es,* or *-ies.*

  the <u>women's</u> dresses   the <u>sheep's</u> fields

A Write the possessive form of each underlined plural noun.

1. <u>wives</u> clubs
2. <u>lawyers</u> cases
3. <u>leaders</u> meetings
4. <u>guinea pigs</u> teeth
5. <u>mice</u> tails
6. <u>moose</u> hooves
7. <u>houses</u> doors

Write the possessive form of each underlined plural noun.

8. Our <u>Presidents</u> lives have all been very different.
9. These <u>men</u> ages and beliefs have also varied.
10. Their <u>families</u> lives have often been hectic.
11. The Roosevelt <u>children</u> pets included mice and rats.
12. One day it will be <u>women</u> turn to lead our country.

B Write *C* if the underlined plural possessive noun is correct. If it is not correct, write the correct form.

1. Politicians campaign to win all the <u>citizen's</u> votes.

2. Our 50 <u>states'</u> elected officials meet in Washington.

3. They work to represent the <u>voters's</u> interests.

4. The <u>senators</u> place of business is the Senate Chamber.

5. The <u>representatives'</u> workplace is the House Chamber.

6. These <u>politician's</u> homes are often far away from Washington.

7. They can't always take part in their <u>children's</u> lives.

8. They all must balance their jobs with their <u>families</u> needs.

9. Often their problems are the same as other <u>men's</u> and <u>womens'</u> problems.

C Complete the sentences with possessive forms of nouns in the box. Write the sentences.

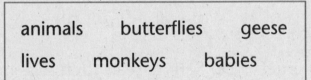

| animals | butterflies | geese |
| lives | monkeys | babies |

10. People need to escape from their ___ busy routines.

11. When I need a change, I go to the zoo and study all the different ___ routines.

12. It is a pleasure just to look at tiny ___ wings.

13. The ___ games and antics make me laugh.

14. Once I saw three large ___ nests by the side of a pond.

15. I could stand at the window of the animal ___ nursery for hours.

Test Preparation

✓ Write the letter of the plural possessive noun that completes each sentence.

1. ___ lives were difficult many years ago.

   A Sailors'   **C** Sailor's
   B Sailor   **D** Sailors

2. Sailing ___ quarters were cramped and smelly.

   A ship's   **C** ship
   B ships'   **D** ships

3. These ___ jobs were hard.

   A mens'   **C** men
   B mans'   **D** men's

4. Not obeying their ___ orders might lead to cruel punishment.

   A officer   **C** officers'
   B officers's **D** officers

5. The ___ fury sometimes threatened their lives.

   A wave'   **C** waves'
   B waves's   **D** wave's

6. Sailors often missed their ___ company.

   A childs'   **C** children
   B childrens' **D** children's

7. In port they eagerly opened their ___ letters.

   A wife's   **C** wifes'
   B wives'   **D** wives

8. Children and home were these ___ world.

   A womens'   **C** women
   B womans'   **D** women's

9. Sailors read their ___ news.

   A families' **C** familys
   B familys'   **D** families

10. Letters home told about foreign ___ sights.

    A countrys'   **C** country's
    B country   **D** countries'

Review

✓ Write the possessive form of each underlined plural noun.

1. <u>drivers</u> cars
2. <u>highways</u> costs
3. <u>deer</u> right-of-way
4. <u>geese</u> crossing
5. <u>pedestrians</u> safety
6. <u>trucks</u> weights
7. <u>babies</u> car seats
8. <u>cities</u> traffic

✓ If the underlined word is written correctly, write *C*. If it is incorrect, write it correctly.

9. Angela Chu designs <u>ladys'</u> clothing.
10. Many <u>countries'</u> fashionable stores stock her products.
11. Her <u>dresses</u> colors are bright and bold.
12. She says that <u>sheep's</u> curly coats have inspired some of her designs.
13. Recently she has started making <u>childrens'</u> clothes.
14. Kids love her t-shirts painted with colorful <u>mices'</u> pawprints.
15. Angela always asks for her <u>customers</u> thoughts.
16. Fashion <u>writers's</u> opinions do not matter to her.
17. She wants to hear <u>womens'</u> ideas about her designs.
18. She is also concerned about her factory <u>workers'</u> health and happiness.

Writing Good Paragraphs

A **good paragraph** often has a topic sentence that clearly states the main idea. It also includes details that support the main idea. Good paragraphs have transitional words that show relationships between ideas, sentences, or paragraphs. Here are some transitions:

Time first, then, next, before, finally, at last, later

Compare/Contrast however, but, although, like

Example for example, namely, that is, along with

Sentences A and B are topic sentences for two paragraphs. Sentences 1 to 7 are supporting details in the paragraphs. Write the letter of the topic sentence that each detail supports.

A To make a campfire first collect the right fuel.

B The second step is to construct the fire.

1. Put the smallest twigs and bits of bark in the center.

2. Collect only dry material.

3. Look for birch bark and fallen pine needles.

4. Place sticks the size of a pencil on top of the bark.

5. Start by finding a flat, clear, dry patch of ground.

6. Dry leaves make excellent kindling.

7. Build up the wood into a teepee shape.

Write a paragraph using this topic sentence: *The second step is to construct the fire.* Use the supporting details you identified. Put them in order and add a transition.

Writing for Tests

Prompt Think of <u>something you like to do</u>. It may be teaching your dog tricks, playing piano, or helping your mother cook. Think about <u>why you like to do this activity</u>. Write <u>two or three well-organized paragraphs</u> explaining your interest to <u>friends or family members</u>.

A strong topic sentence introduces the subject.

Details support the main idea.

Transitions connect paragraphs or ideas within a paragraph.

An effective final sentence sums up the explanation.

Soccer Fever

I've always loved playing soccer. When the weather grows cool in the fall, I get soccer fever. I love the smell of the grass and the sound of the bouncing ball. I even love getting covered in mud. Just put me out on a soccer field, and I'll be happy.

Another reason I have soccer fever is that all my friends play. In fact, soccer practice is like a big party! Everyone I know is running around out there.

The best thing about soccer, though, is that no one tells me I'm wasting my time. For example, if I watched TV all afternoon, my mom would nag me to do something else. Soccer makes everyone happy!

Action and Linking Verbs

The main word in the predicate of a sentence is a verb. Words that show actions are called **action verbs.** Most action verbs show actions you can see. Some action verbs, such as *think* and *understand,* show actions you cannot see.

Action Verbs   Mr. Bailey <u>hit</u> a stranger with his truck.
He <u>regretted</u> the accident.

Linking verbs do not show actions. They tell what the subject is or what the subject is like. Common linking verbs are forms of the verb *to be,* such as *am, is, are, was,* and *were.* Verbs such as *seem, appear, become,* and *feel* can also be linking verbs.

Linking Verbs   The man <u>was</u> alive.
He <u>seemed</u> very strange.

A Write the verb in each sentence.

1. The Bailey family lived on a farm.

2. Mr. Bailey struck a man with his truck.

3. He brought the man home.

4. The stranger was silent.

5. He appeared completely healthy.

6. The stranger changed the weather.

7. Animals trusted the strange man.

8. One morning the stranger disappeared.

B Write *A* if the underlined verb is an action verb. Write *L* if it is a linking verb.

1. March <u>is</u> a great time of year in New England.
2. In the fields, the snow <u>melts</u> into muddy puddles.
3. Little streams <u>become</u> swollen with water.
4. A brisk wind <u>chases</u> the clouds across the sky.
5. Birds <u>return</u> from their winter homes in the south.
6. Green shoots <u>poke</u> their way through the dead leaves.
7. The sun <u>feels</u> warmer every day.
8. A hint of summer <u>fills</u> the air.
9. I <u>open</u> my bedroom window.
10. Now the world <u>seems</u> fresh and new.

C Choose verbs to fill the blanks in the paragraph. When the letter in ( ) is *A*, write an action verb. When the letter is *L*, write a linking verb. Do not use the same verb twice.

(11) My friend John ____ (L) crazy about nature. **(12)** He ____ (A) the plants and animals in the woods near his home. **(13)** Often he quietly ____ (A) birds with his binoculars. **(14)** Once he ____ (A) a beaver dam in the stream. **(15)** When he talks about what he has seen, John ____ (L) very excited. **(16)** Some people find the woods scary, but John ____ (L) content when he is out by himself in the natural world.

Test Preparation

 Write the letter of the verb that completes each sentence.

1. A big maple tree ___ in our backyard.

   A be   **C** standing

   B grows   **D** from

2. It ___ at least 100 years old.

   A do   **C** is

   B until   **D** lasting

3. In summer we ___ in its shade.

   A play   **C** am

   B happy   **D** under

4. Birds ___ nests in its leafy branches.

   A flying   **C** safe

   B noisy   **D** build

 Write the letter of the action or linking verb in each sentence.

5. Our tree's leaves turn golden yellow in October.

   A tree's   **C** golden

   B leaves   **D** turn

6. The leaves float to the ground like orange snow.

   A float   **C** ground

   B to   **D** snow

7. The tree becomes a bare gray skeleton.

   A bare   **C** becomes

   B gray   **D** skeleton

8. The warmth of spring gives our old tree new life at last.

   A last   **C** spring

   B gives   **D** warmth

Review

☑ Write the verb in each sentence. Write *A* if the verb is an action verb. Write *L* if it is a linking verb.

1. Last spring I planted a bean in a flowerpot.
2. A green sprout pushed through the soil a few days later.
3. The bean formed two big leaves.
4. The little plant grew rapidly.
5. In a few weeks, my bean was ready for the garden.
6. I put it in a sunny spot.
7. The bean seemed happy in its new home.
8. It climbed up a long pole.
9. My bean plant became tall and strong.
10. Now it is over six feet high!

☑ Read the label telling the type of verb that is required. Then write the phrase in ( ) that correctly completes the sentence.

11. Action: The tree (blew wildly in the wind, is tall and strong).
12. Linking: The squirrels (raced across the street, were ready for winter).
13. Linking: The river (seems deeper than last year, overflows its banks every spring).
14. Action: The air (felt warm and sticky, hardly moved at all).
15. Linking: Summer (is a time for simple pleasures, often brings hot and humid weather).

Powerful Verbs

If you use forms of the verb *to be* (*am, is, are, was, were*) too often, your writing will sound dull. When other common verbs, such as *say, go,* and *get,* are used frequently, they also can bore a reader. Try replacing these words with **powerful verbs** to create clearer pictures and improve your style.

Weak   The stranger <u>was</u> afraid.
            He <u>went</u> outside.

Strong The stranger <u>trembled</u>.
            He <u>stumbled</u> outside.

Choose a word from the box to replace each underlined word.

Words for *said*	groaned, shouted
Words for *went*	dashed, staggered

1. The injured man <u>went</u> to the farmhouse.
2. "Help me," he <u>said</u>.
3. "Come quickly!" the farmer's wife <u>said</u> to her husband.
4. The farmer <u>went</u> to see what was the matter.

Write two or three sentences about the weather. Use powerful verbs in your description.

Description

> A **description** comes alive with exact nouns, powerful verbs, and details that appeal to the senses. Like all good writing, a description requires a strong beginning and end.

Winter's World

Strong opening catches the reader's interest. —

Where we live, winter arrives like a thief. You don't see him, but you know he's been there. The flowers are gone from the backyard. And where are the tomatoes that were in the big pot on the porch? They're gone too. Winter has stolen them.

As time passes, winter grows bolder. He turns the water in our birdbath into ice. He

Powerful verbs appeal to the senses. —

chases the leaves from the trees. He sneaks through our windows, and we huddle under blankets.

Time-order words help organize the writing.

Finally, winter simply takes over. We look out one day and see a carpet of snow. That's winter's way of saying, "I'm going to stay for a while."

Winter thinks he's won, but we know better. Just wait until spring and see who gets the last laugh!

Main and Helping Verbs

A verb that has more than one word is called a **verb phrase.** A verb phrase is made up of a **main verb** and one or more **helping verbs.** The main verb shows action. The helping verb or verbs tell more about the action. Common helping verbs are *am, is, are, was, were, will, would, should, has, have, had, do, does, can, could, should,* and *would.* In the following sentences, the main verb is underlined once and the helping verb is underlined twice.

A whale <u>has</u> <u>visited</u> our community again.

It <u>was</u> <u>swimming</u> under the boat.

The helping verbs *am, is,* and *are* show present time. *Was* and *were* show past time. *Will* shows future time. The helping verbs *has, have,* and *had* show an action started in the past. Notice the helping verbs in these sentences.

Whales <u>have</u> <u>returned</u> to this bay every year.

The whales <u>will</u> <u>continue</u> their journey north.

A Write the verb phrase in each sentence.

1. The whales are playing in the bay.

2. One whale is swimming near a boat.

3. Many people could visit the bay.

4. They will learn about whales.

5. More visitors have arrived in buses.

6. Everybody is taking photographs.

B Write the part of the verb named in ( ).

   1. Our class has visited the zoo every year. (helping)

   2. Ms. Bond will accompany us again this year. (helping)

   3. We can see the baby gorilla. (helping)

   4. Last year he was clinging to his mother. (main)

   5. He has grown in the last year. (main)

   6. I could watch him all day. (helping)

   7. The elephants were spraying each other. (main)

   8. They do enjoy their showers! (helping)

   9. They can turn their noses into hoses! (main)

10. My grandparents have given me a camera. (main)

11. I am reading the instruction manual. (helping)

12. We should go on a field trip every week. (helping)

13. That would make school more fun. (main)

C Write the sentences. Use words from the box to complete the verb phrases. Use each verb form only once.

can	should	was	show	returned

(14) Recently, my family has ___ from a trip to Hawaii.

(15) You ___ find so much to do there.

(16) While my mom and dad were sunbathing, I ___ learning to surf on the huge waves.

(17) I will ___ you my photographs if you come over tonight. **(18)** You ___ go to Hawaii yourself some day.

Test Preparation

 Write the letter of the helping verb in each sentence.

1. My mom has fed the birds in our backyard all winter.

   A mom   **C** has

   B birds   **D** winter

3. That chickadee would like a turn too.

   A turn   **C** like

   B too   **D** would

2. Two sparrows are eating seeds from our feeder.

   A our   **C** are

   B two   **D** eating

4. Many birds will eat peanut butter.

   A eat   **C** peanut

   B Many   **D** will

 Write the letter of the main verb in each sentence.

5. I am making a bird box.

   A making   **C** box

   B am   **D** bird

7. Birds can build nests there.

   A can   **C** there

   B build   **D** nests

6. Next summer I will nail it to a tree.

   A will   **C** tree

   B Next   **D** nail

8. It should last many years.

   A last   **C** years

   B many   **D** should

Review

✓ Write *helping verb*, *main verb*, or *verb phrase* to identify the underlined words.

1. We were <u>standing</u> there for an hour.

2. My feet <u>are</u> growing cold.

3. I hope the deer <u>will</u> come out soon.

4. Dad said we <u>would see</u> them at sunset.

5. Now it is <u>becoming</u> dark.

6. I <u>am</u> getting impatient.

7. I <u>can</u> hear a noise.

8. A big deer <u>has walked</u> into the open.

✓ Complete the paragraph by creating verb phrases with the helping and main verbs in the box. Use each verb only once.

Helping Verbs		Main Verbs	
have	has	swimming	hoping
can	will	show	try
were	should	watched	laughed
would	am	catch	stop

(**9**) My friend Bob ___ fish with his bare hands. (**10**) I ___ ___ him pull a trout out of the water without a rod or net. (**11**) Several fish ___ ___ close to shore that day. (**12**) Bob promised he ___ ___ me how to do it.

(**13**) I ___ ___ it next weekend. (**14**) Our friend Joyce ___ ___ at the idea. (**15**) I ___ ___ for fresh fish Saturday night. (**16**) That ___ ___ her laughter!

Choosing Details

Choosing details is an important part of writing. Specific details make your narratives, letters, and descriptions come alive. They can make the difference between dull writing and exciting writing.

Without Details   The smell of the sea can be bad at low tide.

With Details   Low tide smells of damp weeds, salty mud, and dead fish.

Read the numbered details. Write the letter of the scene you would match with each detail.

    A Sunrise in a clearing in the mountains

    B A big city on a hot summer night

1. the thudding of a car's stereo

2. the fragrance of pine needles

3. the tinkle of water tumbling over rocks

4. a huge "Open" sign flashing on and off

5. the wail of a police siren

6. fog slowly lifting off the still surface of a pond

List details that you might include in a description about one of these places: the beach, a forest, a city park, a riverbank.

Friendly Letter

A **friendly letter** is exactly what it sounds like. It is a letter written in a friendly voice, often to someone you know well. After writing a friendly letter, ask yourself, "Does my writing sound the way I talk?"

Letter to Adelina

April 10, 2____

Dear Adelina,

Writer uses a friendly tone. —— I've just been reading about your village and all the whales. La Laguna sounds like such an amazing place! Do you think you'll live there all your life?

Where I come from is so different. First of all, I live on the top floor of a big house in a city. When you go out at La Laguna, you see the ocean. When I go out, I see trucks, buses, fire engines, and many cars. You hear the waves and smell the sea. Details catch the reader's interest. —— I hear sirens and smell car exhaust and doughnuts from Linda's Bakery. On Saturday nights the restaurant next door plays music so loud I can't get to sleep!

A cheerful closing ends the letter. —— One day maybe I'll visit La Laguna. Until then, take care of those whales.

Your friend,

Kendra

Subject-Verb Agreement

The subject and the verb in a sentence must work together, or **agree.** To make most present tense verbs agree with singular nouns or *he, she,* or *it,* add -*s* or -*es.* If the subject is a plural noun or *I, you, we,* or *they,* the present tense verb does not end in -*s.*

Singular Subjects	Night <u>follows</u> day. <u>He</u> <u>watches</u> the sunset.
Plural Subjects	<u>Nights</u> <u>give</u> us darkness. <u>We</u> <u>light</u> a candle. <u>Night and day</u> <u>differ</u> greatly.

Use *is* or *was* to agree with singular nouns. Use *are* or *were* to agree with plural nouns. Use *am* to agree with *I.*

Singular Subjects	<u>Night</u> <u>is</u> cool and dark.
Plural Subjects	The night <u>beasts</u> <u>are</u> free.

A Write *Yes* if the subject and the verb in each sentence agree. Write *No* if the subject and the verb do not agree.

1. Some stories tells about natural events.

2. This story explains night and day.

3. Three men travels to the depths of the sea.

Write the verb that correctly completes each sentence.

4. Iemanjá's daughter (love, loves) the night.

5. Flowers (open, opens) their petals in the darkness.

6. An owl (cry, cries) out from a high tree.

B Write *C* if the subject and verb in each sentence agree. If they do not agree, write the verb in the correct form.

1. Earth rotate slowly on its axis.
2. The sun lightens the side of Earth nearer to it.
3. Darkness are on the side of Earth away from the sun.
4. Earth looks like a blue ball from outer space.
5. Astronauts marvels at the beauty of their distant home.
6. White clouds swirls over the oceans.
7. We circles the sun once every year.
8. The other planets move in their own orbits.
9. Mars and Venus is our neighbors in the solar system.
10. I loves to watch the sky at night.

C Expand each subject and verb into an interesting sentence. Use the present-tense form of the verb that agrees with each subject. Remember to begin sentences with a capital letter and end them with a period.

11. night (come)
12. he (make)
13. days (go)
14. I (be)
15. sun (get)
16. Marlon and Leon (carry)

Test Preparation

✓ Mark the letter of the verb that completes each sentence.

1. My little brother Sam ___ afraid of the dark.

   A is   **C** are

   B be   **D** does

2. Scary creatures ___ in the attic, according to Sam.

   A lives   **C** living

   B live   **D** be living

3. They ___ him at night.

   A visits   **C** visiting

   B visites   **D** visit

4. Sam ___ for monsters from under his pillow.

   A watch   **C** watches

   B watchs   **D** watching

5. He ___ them above his head at night.

   A hear   **C** am hearing

   B hearing **D** hears

6. I ___ Sam that noisy squirrels are in the attic.

   A tells   **C** tell

   B telling   **D** tolds

7. Darkness ___ perfectly natural and not something fearful.

   A be   **C** are

   B is   **D** were

8. It ___ not bring monsters to life.

   A do   **C** does

   B done   **D** doing

Review

✓ Write the verb in ( ) that agrees with the subject.

1. Maria (enjoy, enjoys) good stories.
2. She (read, reads) many books.
3. Maria and Juana (go, goes) to the library.
4. Librarians (find, finds) books for them.
5. The girls (show, shows) the books to their parents.
6. Sometimes I (tell, tells) Maria and Juana about other good books.

✓ Write C if the verb in each sentence agrees with its subject. If it does not agree, write the correct form.

7. A myth is a special type of story.
8. It tell about the world long ago.
9. Certain myths explains things.
10. Many famous stories describe the creation of the world.
11. I enjoys myths from other cultures.
12. We read myths and legends in school.
13. Some legends involves real characters.
14. Giants and heroes is the subjects of legends.
15. King Arthur were a legendary character.
16. Myths and legends fascinates me.

Similes and Metaphors

> **Similes** and **metaphors** are figures of speech that compare two unlike things. A simile uses the word *like* or *as* when making the comparison, while a metaphor does not.
>
> **Simile**   The sky at night is like a city.
> **Metaphor** The sky at night is a city.
>
> By creating strong, unusual comparisons, similes and metaphors make readers look at things differently.

Read the paragraph. Each numbered sentence contains either a simile or a metaphor. Identify the figures of speech.

   (1) My heart was pounding like a drum. I was on stage for the first time, and I had to sing. What was I going to do? I wasn't a six-year-old boy anymore. **(2)** I was a scared rabbit, and I wanted to run. I tried to take Dad's advice. "Be strong," he said. **(3)** "Remember, you're a rock." But I didn't feel like a rock. **(4)** I was a balloon about to pop.

For each of the subjects below, think of a simile or metaphor. Write a sentence using your idea.

   5. A calm pond
   6. A big storm
   7. An angry person
   8. A hot day

Comparisons

> When you want a reader to look at something a little differently, you might write a comparison. **Comparisons** take two different things and show how they are alike. Good comparisons may use figures of speech such as similes or metaphors to make their point.

Opening question catches reader's attention. ———

Similes and metaphors create the comparison. ———

Short topic sentences sum up main ideas. ———

New idea at the end makes reader think. ———

The City of the Sky

Have you ever been outside at night in the country? A funny thing happens when you are far from the city lights. The sky becomes a city. It's as if you are in an airplane, looking down instead of up. All of those stars and planets are lights in the City of the Sky.

The City of the Sky is alive. Watch a star closely and you'll see that it twinkles. There's traffic in the city too. Keep on watching, and you'll see airplanes, satellites, and maybe a shooting star.

There's much activity in the city. Scientists say that there are billions of worlds up there. They whirl and spin millions of light years away.

I wonder if somewhere in the City of the Sky there are people like me.

Past, Present, and Future Tenses

The **tense** of a verb tells when an action happens. A verb in the **present tense** tells about action that is happening now. A verb in the **past tense** tells about action that has already happened. Many past tense verbs end in *-ed*. A verb in the **future tense** tells about action that will happen in the future. The helping verb *will* is added to a verb to form the future tense.

Present Tense	The rain <u>pours</u>. We <u>use</u> umbrellas.
Past Tense	It <u>rained</u> last night. We <u>waded</u> in puddles.
Future Tense	The rain <u>will stop</u> tomorrow.

- When a verb ends with *e,* drop the *e* before adding *-ed: save/saved.*

- When a one-syllable verb ends with one vowel followed by one consonant, double the final consonant before adding *-ed: clap/clapped.*

- When a verb ends with a consonant followed by *y,* change the *y* to *i* before adding *-ed: hurry/hurried.*

A Write *present, past,* or *future* for each underlined verb.

1. My dog <u>hates</u> thunderstorms.

2. He <u>hides</u> under the bed during a storm.

3. Last summer a storm <u>arrived</u> one afternoon.

4. The wind nearly <u>knocked</u> me over.

5. Next time I <u>will stay</u> indoors.

B Write the underlined verb in each sentence in the tense shown in ( ). Write the sentence.

1. My family <u>take</u> a summer vacation every year. (present)

2. We often <u>visit</u> beautiful places. (present)

3. Last summer we <u>camp</u> in a state forest. (past)

4. It <u>rain</u> for six days. (past)

5. We <u>worry</u> about our leaky tent. (past)

6. Water <u>drip</u> on our heads. (past)

7. We <u>shiver</u> in the cold. (past)

8. Dad <u>look</u> for different vacation spots each year. (present)

9. Next summer we <u>rent</u> a cabin. (future)

10. A solid roof <u>keep</u> us dry. (future)

C Complete the paragraph with verbs from the box. Put each verb in past or future tense as necessary.

close	melt	play	rain
shine	snow	stop	change

My sister Sarah and I love winter weather. **(11)** We were happy last week because it ___ for 24 hours. **(12)** All the traffic in town ___. **(13)** Our school ___ at noon. **(14)** Sarah and I ___ outside all afternoon. **(15)** Unfortunately, the weather ___ tomorrow. **(16)** The forecasters predict that it ___. **(17)** After that, the sun ___. **(18)** Our poor snowman ___.

Test Preparation

 Write the letter of the verb that completes each sentence.

1. Pedro's mom ___ him home from school most days.

   A drived   **C** drive

   B driving   **D** drives

2. Normally the trip ___ five minutes.

   A takes   **C** take

   B taking   **D** taked

3. One day last year Pedro ___ for his mom at the front door.

   A will wait   **C** waited

   B wait   **D** waitd

4. When she arrived, Pedro ___ to the car.

   A hurry's   **C** hurried

   B hurryed   **D** hurreed

5. Just before he got there, a tree branch ___ down on the car.

   A will crash   **C** crasht

   B crash   **D** crashed

6. The branch ___ Pedro's mom inside the car.

   A trapped   **C** trappied

   B traped   **D** trappt

7. Firefighters ___ her.

   A rescued   **C** rescewd

   B rescueed   **D** rescues

8. Pedro's mom ___ insurance money for the car next month.

   A collected   **C** collect

   B will collect   **D** collecting

Review

✓ Write the verb in each sentence. Then write whether it is *past*, *present*, or *future*.

1. Earth's climate changes over the centuries.
2. Sometimes it gets warmer.
3. The polar ice caps retreat in warm periods.
4. Tropical plants grow in the northern forests.
5. During the last Ice Age, glaciers covered Canada.
6. Many animals died in the cold.
7. Today many scientists predict another change.
8. Our climate will become much warmer.
9. The ice caps will melt.
10. Ocean levels will rise.
11. Millions of people will lose their homes.
12. No one knows the future for sure, of course.

✓ Complete the sentences by writing the underlined verb in the tense in ( ). If no change is necessary, write *NC*.

13. I love all kinds of stormy weather. (present)
14. Long ago, I beg to go out in the rain. (past)
15. I hop over puddles. (past)
16. I race to school. (past)
17. I try to catch snowflakes in my mouth. (past)
18. I still enjoy rain, sleet, and snow. (present)
19. Perhaps tomorrow it sleet. (future)
20. I go outdoors and enjoy it. (future)

Organization

When you write, put your ideas in an order that makes sense. **Organization**—the way ideas are arranged—is like the skeleton of a body. It holds your writing together. Here are some ways to organize your writing.

- Story with a beginning, middle, and end
- Compare-contrast
- Step-by-step explanation
- Description from top to bottom or left to right

Words help organize your writing too. Time-order words such as *first, next, tomorrow,* and *finally* show sequence. Connecting words such as *but, however, too,* and *also* show differences and likenesses.

Each numbered item below is the title of a writing assignment. Write the letter of the kind of organization that would be best for that assignment.

A Story   **C** Step-by-step explanation

B Comparison-contrast   **D** Description

1. Why Winter Is Better than Summer

2. How to Make the Best Brownies

3. What Happened on My First Day of School

4. Directions to My House

5. Portrait of Grandpa

Problem/Solution

> **Problem/solution** writing describes a problem and then tells how the problem was solved or can be solved. When describing a solution, the writer must be well organized. Time-order words such as *first*, *then*, and *finally* help readers understand the explanation.

Opening exclamation catches reader's attention. ——

Writer clearly explains the problem. ——

Sequence words help explain the solution. ——

Ending ties back to opening. ——

A Key to the Solution

"Oops!" I said.

The key slipped from my hand and fell through a gap in the floorboards. I was standing on my front porch. The door was locked, and my mom was away. I was stuck. "Uh-oh," I thought.

Have you ever had a brainstorm? That's when a light bulb goes off in your head. At that moment, I remembered an old science project on magnets. It was still in our garage. First I found a magnet and tied it to a string. Then I lowered the magnet through the crack until it nudged the key. Click! The magnet grabbed the key. Very slowly, I pulled up the string. I held my breath until I had the key safely in my hands again.

"Wow!" I said.

Irregular Verbs

Usually you add *-ed* to a verb to show past tense.
Irregular verbs change in other ways.

Present Tense	Men <u>come</u> here.
Past Tense	Men <u>came</u> here.
Past with *has, have,* or *had*	Men <u>have come</u> here.

Irregular verbs have a special form when they are used
with *has, have,* or *had*. Below are some examples.

Present Tense	Past Tense	Past with *has, have,* or *had*
come	came	(*has, have, had*) come
fall	fell	(*has, have, had*) fallen
go	went	(*has, have, had*) gone
hear	heard	(*has, have, had*) heard
hit	hit	(*has, have, had*) hit
is/are	was/were	(*has, have, had*) been
leave	left	(*has, have, had*) left
read	read	(*has, have, had*) read
see	saw	(*has, have, had*) seen
take	took	(*has, have, had*) taken
tell	told	(*has, have, had*) told
write	wrote	(*has, have, had*) written

A Write the past tense of each irregular verb.

1. go
2. leave
3. hit
4. fall
5. come
6. take

B Write the correct past form of the verb in ( ).

1. I have (read) a book about how animals communicate.
2. We (see) a movie about a gorilla that knew sign language.
3. Our teacher has (tell) us about her talking parrot.
4. An expert on dolphins (come) to our school.
5. We (hear) a tape recording of whale noises.
6. My brother has (write) a paper about bird songs.
7. That paper (take) a long time to complete.
8. The whole class (go) to the science museum yesterday.
9. We (leave) at 7 A.M. to get there by 9.
10. I have (is/are) to the zoo several times.

C Complete the story with verbs from the box. Put each verb in the past tense or the past tense with *has, have,* or *had.*

come	fall	is/are	leave
see	take	tell	write

(11) Now I have ___ everything! **(12)** If anyone had ___ me this, I probably wouldn't have believed them. Here's what happened. **(13)** I had ___ soccer practice Monday and was walking home. **(14)** On the corner of Spring and Elm, this black cat ___ up to me and looked me straight in the eyes. **(15)** "I have ___ waiting to speak to you," the cat said. **(16)** As you can imagine, I nearly ___ over. **(17)** It must have ___ me a few seconds to get over my surprise. When I looked again, the cat had vanished. **(18)** I have ___ about this event in my journal.

Test Preparation

 Write the letter of the verb that correctly completes each sentence.

1. Europeans have ___ in America for over 400 years.

   A been   **C** ben
   B be   **D** bin

2. The first settlers who ___ here were astonished.

   A come   **C** comed
   B came   **D** coming

3. They ___ endless forests.

   A seen   **C** sawed
   B seed   **D** saw

4. They ___ the cries of wolves and eagles.

   A heared   **C** heard
   B herd   **D** hearing

5. Families ___ the coast and traveled west.

   A leaved   **C** leave
   B leafed   **D** left

6. They had ___ across prairies and mountains.

   A gone   **C** went
   B goed   **D** goned

7. They ___ about their new homes.

   A wroted   **C** wrote
   B writed   **D** written

8. In class we have ___ their descriptions.

   A read   **C** reading
   B red   **D** readed

Review

✓ Write the verb form in ( ) that correctly completes each sentence.

1. Late last night I (heard, hearing) a scratching noise.
2. "Who has (came, come) to see me at this hour?" I wondered.
3. The door opened, but I (saw, seen) no one.
4. On the floor (were, be) a mousetrap and a tiny note.
5. I picked up the note and (read, readed) it.
6. "How would you like it if we (leaved, left) a trap for you?" the note said.

✓ Write the correct past form of the verb in ( ).

7. Long ago a huge meteor (fall) to Earth.
8. It (hit) our planet near Mexico.
9. The meteor (leave) many creatures extinct.
10. This (is/are) a terrible disaster.
11. The sky (go) dark.
12. It (take) millions of years for Earth to recover.
13. We have (read) about this event in science class.
14. Many scientists have (write) about it.
15. Imagine if someone had (take) photographs!
16. Since then many meteors have (come) to Earth.
17. I have (hear) that a huge meteor once struck Russia.
18. None of these later meteors have (is/are) as big.

Dialogue

Dialogue is the words that characters say to each other. The reader knows that these words are spoken because they are inside quotation marks ("/"). Good writing often includes dialogue. Characters' speech helps bring a story to life.

Choose items from the box that best complete the dialogue below. Write the sentences with correct punctuation.

> Where has all the good grass gone
> I lost my tail in a trap
> Something must be done about people
> Their factories are poisoning my water
> The air is too smoky for me to fly

1. "___!" all the animals shouted.

2. "___," announced a fish.

3. "___," added an eagle.

4. "___?" asked a cow.

5. The small, squeaky voice of a mouse chimed in, "___!"

Imagine that it is your birthday. Write a short dialogue with two characters in which you open a gift. Let the reader know how you feel from what you say.

Writing for Tests

> **Prompt** Imagine that <u>an animal or something else in nature</u>—perhaps a tree, rock, or river—<u>could speak</u> to people. What would it tell us or warn us about? Write <u>a fantasy of several paragraphs</u> describing what this thing or creature says. Include <u>dialogue</u> in your fantasy.

Words of Warning

Direct quotations are correctly punctuated.

I don't suppose anyone will believe this. When I told my mom, she just said, "You've been dreaming, Jason." But I wasn't. Here's what happened.

Writer sets scene.

Last Monday I was down at the construction site where they're building the new mall. Two sparrows were twittering on the fence nearby. It was weird, but suddenly I could understand what they were saying.

Dialogue gives exact words spoken.

"They're doing it again," one sparrow said.

"It's always the same," the other replied. "Men and women think that they can kill the trees and flowers and get away with it."

"They'll learn an awful lesson," the first bird said.

"What lesson?" I shouted. But the birds flew away.

Ending gets reader involved.

I'm not kidding, and I wasn't dreaming. I heard every word those sparrows said. What do you think they meant?

Singular and Plural Pronouns

Pronouns are words that take the place of nouns.
Singular pronouns take the place of singular nouns.
I, me, he, she, him, her, and *it* are singular pronouns.
Plural pronouns take the place of plural nouns. *We, us, they,* and *them* are plural pronouns.

The <u>man</u> met <u>the magicians</u> at the train station.

<u>He</u> met <u>them</u> at the train station.

Always capitalize the singular pronoun *I*. When you talk about yourself and another person, name yourself last. The pronoun *you* can be singular or plural.

A Write the pronoun in each sentence.

1. I want to learn more about Harry Houdini.
2. He was a famous magician.
3. Tell us about Houdini's tricks.
4. Houdini got into a crate and had it lowered into the ocean.
5. People were amazed when they saw Houdini escape.
6. You would enjoy reading about Houdini.
7. We gave Mom a book about the magician.
8. Mom took the Houdini book with her to Indiana.
9. She read the book on the train ride.
10. When people asked, Mom told them about the magician's amazing deeds.

B Write the pronoun in each sentence. Then write *S* if the pronoun is singular or *P* if it is plural.

1. The sky was dark, and it looked like rain.
2. "What shall we do this afternoon?" Louis wondered.
3. "Do you have any suggestions, Marcus?" Louis asked.
4. Then he got a great idea.
5. "Help me stage a magic show," Louis said.
6. "Mary Alice will probably help us too."
7. "She has magic cards and an invisible cloak."
8. "You both can do tricks for the show," Marcus said.

C Revise each pair of sentences. Replace underlined words with a singular or plural pronoun from the box.

him	she	us	they

9. Victor's mother does not know what to do with Victor. Victor's mother worries constantly.
10. Victor wants to be a magician like Houdini. Houdini's tricks have greatly impressed Victor.
11. Mother and Victor went to see Victor's Aunt Harriet. Mother and Victor showed Aunt Harriet Victor's tricks.
12. Later, Victor visited Louis and me. He promised to help Louis and me with the magic show.

Test Preparation

☑ Write the letter of the word that completes each sentence in the paragraph.

(1) ____ am Alhambro the great and wonderful! (2) For my first trick, I will have a young lady come to the stage so I can saw ____ in half. (3) Amazingly, ____ will sit down unharmed when I utter the magic words. (4) Then I shall take my wizard's hat and pull ten rabbits from ____. (5) And you will see that ____ all return to the hat.

(6) Are ____ ready to be astonished? (7) Then please give ____ your complete attention. (8) ____ magicians require absolute silence.

1.	A	We	C	He
	B	I	D	They

6.	A	they	C	we
	B	you	D	she

2.	A	you	C	her
	B	us	D	them

7.	A	us	C	you
	B	them	D	me

3.	A	she	C	we
	B	they	D	he

8.	A	He	C	I
	B	Me	D	We

4.	A	us	C	them
	B	it	D	me

5.	A	they	C	he
	B	you	D	it

Review

✓ Write the pronoun in each sentence. Write *S* if the pronoun is singular. Write *P* if it is plural.

1. Dad and I enjoy watching movies together.
2. We watch movies at home on DVDs.
3. Movies with stunts give us a thrill.
4. Stunt people are amazing because they have so much nerve.
5. Mom appreciates them but doesn't want to see any stunts in this house.

✓ Write the pronoun in ( ) that replaces each underlined word or words.

6. Ruth and Sal are learning about special effects. (They, She)
7. The girls spilled a bottle of stage blood on the rug. (it, us)
8. Sal's dad came home at that moment. (They, He)
9. He was furious with the girls. (her, them)
10. The girls helped Sal's father clean the room. (us, him)

✓ Write the pronoun in ( ) that correctly completes each sentence.

11. Jaime and I are going to the school play tonight and hope that you'll come with (him, us).
12. (It, She) is a fantasy about people who can fly.
13. The kids in the cast are attached to steel wires, and (he, they) really seem to be flying.
14. Why don't (I, we) meet at the school this evening?
15. I know that (you, she) are interested in special effects.

Good Beginnings

What happens when you start reading something that seems dull? You probably stop reading! If you want people to read your writing, you need a **good beginning.** Start with a question, an interesting fact, or an exclamation. Look at the examples below.

- Snow is made up of tiny ice crystals that form in the clouds.
- My friends and I like to play in the snow.
- Snowflakes are like the cookies my sister and I make.

Which beginning do you think is most interesting?

Copy the sentence below that would make the best beginning for an article called "Harry Houdini: Escape Artist."

1. Harry Houdini was born in 1874.

2. Imagine being locked in a crate and lying on the ocean floor.

3. I think Houdini was one of the world's greatest magicians.

The sentences below need a good beginning to make them into an effective paragraph. Write two or three sentences that get the paragraph off to a good start.

You can go for walks with a dog, but you can't with a cat. Dogs can retrieve balls, play hide and seek, and shake hands. They know when you are sad or sick. Cats can't do any of these things. That's why dogs are better than cats.

Story about a Discovery

A good story keeps the reader interested from beginning to end. The opening sentence should catch the reader's interest. In **a story about a discovery,** like the one below, it is a good idea not to reveal the actual discovery until the very end.

A good beginning catches reader's interest.

Writer explains his feelings.

Dialogue makes the story realistic.

A discovery rounds off the story.

The Bear Facts

When I was four years old, I went bear hunting with my dad in the basement. My brother had told me about the bears. They ate crumbs that fell through cracks in the kitchen floor. "Don't go down there alone!" he warned me.

I was very scared and very curious. Why hadn't I ever heard the bears clumping around? What if they clumped upstairs?

It was my dad who suggested the hunt. I took a flashlight, and my dad carried a baseball bat. We hunted and hunted, but there were no bears.

"I guess they've moved out," my dad said. "I'll lock the door so they won't get back in."

That's when I discovered that my brother didn't always tell the truth.

Subject and Object Pronouns

A **subject pronoun** is used in the subject of a sentence. Singular subject pronouns are *I, you, he, she,* and *it.* When you use a noun and a pronoun in a compound subject, be sure to use a subject pronoun.

<u>She</u> went to Brazil. Luisa and <u>I</u> stayed home.

Plural subject pronouns are *we, you,* and *they*.

<u>We</u> looked for dolphins. <u>They</u> were hard to see.

An **object pronoun** is used in the predicate of a sentence after an action verb or with a preposition, such as *for, at, about, with,* or *to.* Singular object pronouns are *me, you, him, her,* and *it.*

The dolphin saw <u>her</u>. It looked at Luisa and <u>me</u>.

Plural object pronouns are *us, you,* and *them.* When you use a noun and a pronoun in a compound object, be sure to use an object pronoun.

We saw a whale and <u>them</u>. They swam with <u>us</u>.

Ⓐ Write *SP* if the underlined pronoun is a subject pronoun. Write *OP* if it is an object pronoun.

1. <u>He</u> knows where to find the dolphins.

2. Who saw <u>them</u> first?

3. That dolphin is playing with <u>us</u>.

4. After a day or two, <u>we</u> will visit the dolphins again.

5. Let's photograph Carlos and <u>her</u> in the canoe.

B Write the pronoun in ( ) that completes each sentence.

1. Carla and (I, me) are researching unusual animals.

2. Ms. Sanchez told the boys and (we, us) to select a species.

3. (We, Us) have found many to choose from.

4. Giant squids fascinate Carla and (I, me).

5. Scientists know very little about (they, them).

6. Carla is Australian, and (she, her) wants to study koala bears.

7. (They, Them) look just like stuffed toys.

8. Australian animals interest several other students and (she, her).

9. Al wants a different project for the boys and (he, him).

10. By next Friday, the boys and (we, us) must both make some decisions.

C Add a pronoun to complete each numbered sentence in the paragraph.

(11) When Sam, Ted, and ____ began our project on dinosaurs, we didn't know where to start. (12) ____ seemed like such a big subject. Then Sam had a brainstorm. (13) He explained his idea to Ted and ____.

(14) "Let's write a story," ____ said. (15) "It could be about a boy who finds a baby dinosaur in the woods and takes it home to live with his family and ____! (16) That way ____ can describe what the dinosaur looks like and what it eats."

(17) That sounded like a good idea to ____, so we agreed. That afternoon Sam, Ted and I began writing our book. (18) Many of our friends have asked Ted and ____ how it ends. But Sam has an ending that is still a deep secret.

Test Preparation

Write the letter of the word or words that complete each sentence.

(1) Carlos, Melinda, and ___ are creating a model rainforest. (2) Carlos is an old friend of mine, and Melinda and ___ are cousins. (3) Anyway, this forest has taken ___ two weeks to make so far. (4) The vines are ropes with real leaves stuck to ___. (5) We've made a big snake called Sally and twisted ___ around one of the trees. (6) We recorded the birds in the pet shop, and ___ sound just like rainforest creatures. (7) The principal told Carlos and ___ that he would like to show his family our forest when it is finished. (8) We said we'd protect his children and ___ from dangerous animals!

1. **A** me   **C** I
   B her   **D** us

2. **A** him   **C** her
   B them   **D** he

3. **A** they and I   **C** them and me
   B we   **D** he and her

4. **A** it   **C** they
   B them   **D** him

5. **A** she   **C** he
   B her   **D** they

6. **A** them   **C** they
   B you   **D** him

7. **A** me   **C** she
   B they   **D** I

8. **A** him   **C** we
   B he   **D** they

Review

✓ Write the subject pronoun in each sentence.

1. You and Cindy should watch this show with me.
2. It describes how important rainforests are to us.
3. We get many life-saving medicines from them.
4. People value the forests, but they still chop them down.
5. The show is on late, but I will watch it anyway.

✓ Write the object pronoun in each sentence.

6. Hand me the glue, if you don't mind.
7. This tree has lost a leaf, and I will glue it back on.
8. Making trees was fun, but it was hard work for us.
9. Mr. Bond said that we made them look very realistic.
10. According to him, we deserve a good grade.

✓ Write the pronoun(s) in ( ) that correctly complete each sentence.

11. (Me and Cher, Cher and I) are learning about rainforest birds.
12. This is an important project for (her and me, she and I).
13. (Them, You) can find toucans in some rainforests.
14. Macaws and (they, them) are brightly colored birds.
15. When Mr. Smith visited Costa Rica, a tour guide pointed out colorful birds to (he, him).
16. The tour guide and (he, him) became good friends.

Sensory Details

To bring a description to life, writers use **sensory details.** Sensory details tell how something looks, sounds, smells, tastes, or feels. These kinds of details make writing vivid and real. They help readers experience what the writer is describing.

Sight	the glistening, black surface of the water
Sound	a slow, deep gurgling
Touch	the damp, slippery skin of a frog
Smell	a stench of rotting plants
Taste	sweet, like an overripe banana

Decide which sense the writer is appealing to in each sentence below. Write *sight, sound, touch, smell,* or *taste.*

1. Thousands of trees rose around me like the walls of an enormous green prison.

2. The heat made my skin prickle and burn.

3. Golden sunlight filtered through the leaves.

4. The air was thick with the odor of mud and flowers.

5. My boots sank into the soft, spongy earth.

6. I licked the salty sweat from my lips.

7. A howler monkey shrieked in the branches above.

8. Then the terrible silence returned.

Write a paragraph about a summer day. Use sentences that appeal to at least four of the five senses.

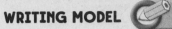

Travel Brochure

A **travel brochure** tries to persuade readers to visit the place it describes. The writer of a travel brochure uses vivid, lively images to bring the place to life.

Opening sentence makes the topic clear.

Vivid images appeal to the senses.

Writer addresses reader directly.

Ending neatly rephrases opening.

A Lake for All Seasons

At any time of year, Lake Marisa is the ideal place for a quiet getaway. Its peaceful waters mirror the deep blue of a summer sky. Only the wild call of a loon breaks the stillness of a summer night.

In the fall, Lake Marisa glitters with red and orange. Paddle along its shores to admire the golden forest and feel the sharp touch of the new season.

Winter brings its own special beauty. The trees are clothed in white, and the lake is a crystal dance floor.

And don't forget the spring. Take time in May to wander on a carpet of bluebells and to smell the fragrance of new life.

Summer, fall, winter, or spring, Lake Marisa has all you need for the perfect break.

Pronouns and Antecedents

A **pronoun** takes the place of a noun or nouns. An **antecedent,** or referent, is the noun or nouns to which the pronoun refers. A pronoun and its antecedent must agree in number and gender.

Before you use a pronoun, ask yourself whether the antecedent is singular or plural. If the antecedent is singular, decide whether it is masculine, feminine, or neuter. Then choose a pronoun that agrees. In the following sentences, the antecedents are underlined once; the pronouns are underlined twice.

The <u>maid</u> was sitting at a table, where <u>she</u> was shelling peas.

The <u>cook and the maid</u> were amazed when <u>they</u> saw the king.

A Match the pronoun with the noun or noun phrase that could be its antecedent. Write the letter.

1. it		**A**	two kitchen maids
2. they		**B**	dungeon
3. we		**C**	the peasant and I

Write the correct pronoun in ( ) to complete each sentence. The antecedents of the pronouns are underlined.

4. Cook spoke to the <u>guard</u> when (he, it) passed by.

5. The <u>King</u> made Cook blindfold (her, him).

B Write a pronoun to replace each underlined noun or noun phrase.

1. My older brother Sal and I decided to bake a cake when <u>Sal and I</u> were home alone one day.

2. Our parents were out, and we wanted to surprise <u>our parents</u>.

3. We cracked two eggs, but <u>the eggs</u> fell on the floor.

4. The flour spilled, and <u>flour</u> went all over the kitchen.

5. Our little brother came in the kitchen, but we told <u>our little brother</u> to leave.

6. Butter started dripping everywhere when we melted <u>the butter</u>.

7. Our parents were not happy with <u>Sal and me</u>.

8. Mom said that <u>Mom</u> would watch us clean up.

9. Dad said that <u>Dad</u> would stay out of the way.

10. Sal said that our parents could put the blame on <u>Sal</u>.

C Write one or two sentences using the sets of words below. Use the first item as the antecedent of the pronoun.

Example   food; it
              I enjoy eating food and cooking it too.

11. Amy, Joel, and I; we
12. cupcakes; them
13. recipe; it
14. cookies; they
15. Amy; she
16. Joel and I; us

Test Preparation

✓ Read the following paragraph. Write the letter of the pronoun that correctly completes each sentence. The antecedents of the pronouns are underlined.

    (1) Why do some people like <u>a certain type of food</u>, while other people hate ____? **(2)** For example, my brother loves <u>olives</u>, but I can't stand ____. **(3)** <u>My sister</u> removes all the cheese when ____ eats a slice of pizza. **(4)** <u>Mom and Dad</u> paid a lot of money to eat black fish eggs when ____ went out to dinner. **(5)** <u>Uncle Norman</u> says that a friend served ____ calves' brains, and they were delicious! **(6)** <u>Aunt Ada</u> said that my uncle won't get brains from ____. **(7)** She said <u>Uncle Norman</u> liked eating brains because ____ doesn't have any himself! **(8)** <u>My relatives and I</u> often disagree about food when ____ get together.

1. **A** them   **C** they
   B us   **D** it

2. **A** them   **C** it
   B him   **D** her

3. **A** it   **C** she
   B I   **D** you

4. **A** us   **C** she
   B they   **D** he

5. **A** it   **C** him
   B them   **D** he

6. **A** it   **C** him
   B her   **D** you

7. **A** she   **C** we
   B he   **D** they

8. **A** I   **C** you
   B they   **D** we

Review

✓ Write the correct pronoun in ( ) to complete each sentence. The antecedents of the pronouns are underlined.

1. <u>Dad</u> says eggs are the food (they, he) likes best.
2. When Dad cooks <u>eggs</u>, he scrambles (it, them).
3. If <u>my brother and I</u> are up early, Dad makes eggs for (us, we).
4. <u>Mom</u> says (she, her) learned to cook eggs to make Dad happy.
5. When <u>Dad</u> has a birthday, we plan to give (it, him) a hen!

✓ Write the antecedent of the underlined pronoun.

6. My sister baked her own birthday cake when <u>she</u> was six.
7. The cake was sweet, but <u>it</u> was chewy like rubber.
8. She invited several friends and served <u>them</u> each a slice.
9. My fork bounced out when I stuck <u>it</u> into the cake.
10. Our dog liked the cake, so we gave most of it to <u>him</u>.

✓ Write a pronoun to replace each underlined noun or noun phrase.

11. You should wash the dishes after every meal and not leave <u>the dishes</u> in the sink.
12. Ben washes dishes after <u>Ben</u> has had his supper.
13. Ben puts on an apron, and his mom ties it behind <u>Ben</u>.
14. He washes glasses first because <u>glasses</u> show the dirt.
15. When Ben's sister is home, <u>Ben's sister</u> helps clean up.

Elaborate

Writing can be unclear if the writer does not **elaborate** on his or her ideas. Exact nouns, strong verbs, and vivid sensory details can make writing fresh and clear.

Before Elaboration	Cook made something.
After Elaboration	Cook prepared a soup that tasted like ditch water.
Before Elaboration	The Princess was happy.
After Elaboration	The Princess shouted for joy and hugged her father.

Replace the underlined word or words with interesting, exact details. Write the new sentence.

1. I like cooking <u>stuff</u>.
2. She baked <u>a nice dessert</u>.
3. The kitchen was full of <u>things</u>.
4. He ate <u>a lot</u>.
5. The kitchen was <u>big</u>.
6. The cake was <u>pretty</u>.
7. The table was <u>set</u>.
8. The salsa <u>was hot</u>.

Make the paragraph below more interesting by elaborating.

   The King did not like his dinner. He was very angry. He went to the kitchen. We were frightened.

Business Letter

A **business letter** is written to an organization or a company. The writer might be buying or selling something, asking for information, or looking for a job. A business letter should be informative, precise, and clear.

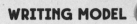

A Very Sticky Business

Dear Sir or Madam:

Opening sentence makes the purpose of the letter clear. — I am writing about a new product I believe could change the world. King's Glue is simple and safe to use, yet strong enough for any job. It can fix a pair of shoes or stick a man's teeth together in an instant, and it costs just pennies to make.

Details elaborate on the opening sentence. — I am presently producing large quantities of King's Glue in the Royal Kitchens. Several vats of it are ready for use. All I need is a partner to help sell it. Will you be that partner?

Request is clearly made. —

Ending sums up proposal and gives contact information. — With my glue and your sales force, we could alter forever the way people stick things together. Please contact me at the Palace if you are interested in this project.

Yours truly,
The King

LESSON 19

Possessive Pronouns

Possessive pronouns show who or what owns, or possesses, something. *My, mine, your, yours, her, hers, his, its, our, ours, their,* and *theirs* are possessive pronouns.

- Use *my, your, her, our,* and *their* before nouns.
  I study at <u>my</u> desk. Experts shared <u>their</u> discoveries.
- Use *mine, yours, hers, ours,* and *theirs* alone.
  The desk is <u>mine</u>. The discoveries were <u>theirs</u>.
- *His* and *its* can be used both before nouns and alone.
  Jean-François did <u>his</u> work. The work was <u>his</u>.
  The alphabet revealed <u>its</u> secrets. The secrets were <u>its</u>.
- Do not use an apostrophe with a possessive pronoun.

A Write the possessive pronoun in each sentence.

   1. Ancient Egyptians left many samples of their writing.

   2. The Egyptian alphabet was very different from ours.

   3. Some of its letters were pictures of animals.

   4. Jean-François Champollion concentrated on his study of them for years.

Write the possessive pronoun in ( ) that completes each sentence.

   5. (Our, Ours) class is studying ancient Egypt.

   6. Julio and Pam made a model of the Rosetta Stone for (their, theirs) presentation.

B Write a possessive pronoun to replace the underlined words or phrases.

1. The secret to the ancient civilization was hidden in <u>the civilization's</u> alphabet.

2. Two experts worked to prove <u>the experts'</u> theories.

3. John Rossi believed that <u>John Rossi's</u> ideas were correct.

4. Mary Chung preferred <u>Mary Chung's</u> ideas.

5. Mary Chung wrote a book about <u>Mary Chung's</u> theory.

6. I believe that space aliens taught <u>the space aliens'</u> alphabet to the ancient people.

7. Most people think that Mary Chung's theory is correct, but <u>Jack's and my</u> theory about aliens is more interesting.

8. Experts have their opinions, Jack and I have one, and you can have <u>one belonging to you</u> too.

C If a sentence contains a possessive pronoun error, rewrite the sentence correcting the error. If a sentence is correct, write *C*.

9. The door creaked on it's hinges.

10. Bill and I turned on their flashlights, and I waited for my heart to stop pounding.

11. Ahead of us was the coffin where the king had his last resting place.

12. Strange symbols decorated its sides, with there paint almost worn off from age.

13. This ancient writing was very different from our.

14. Wouldn't you're heart be beating as wildly as ours if you were in our place?

Test Preparation

✔ Write the letter of the possessive pronoun that correctly completes each sentence.

1. ____ English alphabet has 26 letters.

   A Our   **C** Ours
   B Her   **D** Mine

2. Many other languages have ____ own alphabets.

   A theirs   **C** its
   B their   **D** your

3. I would like to learn another way of writing, but I only know ____.

   A our   **C** our's
   B her   **D** ours

4. Miwako showed me a newspaper from ____ country.

   A its   **C** her
   B theirs   **D** yours

5. I said that I'd help her with our writing if she'd teach me ____.

   A her   **C** her's
   B its   **D** hers

6. Mr. Rey says that people in ____ country tied knots in string.

   A yours   **C** his
   B hers   **D** its

7. Each knot had ____ own special meaning.

   A their   **C** its
   B it's   **D** his

8. I can only tie the knot in ____ shoelaces!

   A my   **C** its
   B mine   **D** yours

Review

✓ Write the possessive pronoun in ( ) that completes each sentence.

1. Many people visit Peru to see (its, it's) Incan ruins.

2. You can read about the Incas in (you're, your) history book.

3. An archaeologist visited (our, ours) school.

4. She had spent years of (hers, her) life studying the Incas.

5. The Incas were famous for (theirs, their) stonework.

6. She compared their buildings to (our, ours).

7. I tried making (my, mine) own Incan stonewall at home.

8. The Inca's walls were well built, but (my, mine) was a mess!

✓ If the underlined possessive pronoun is correct, write *C*. If it is incorrect, write the correct form.

9. My friend George and I write to each other in <u>ours</u> secret code.

10. Each letter has <u>its</u> own symbol.

11. Amy and Song have also invented <u>theirs</u> secret way of writing.

12. Their code is completely different from <u>our</u>.

13. <u>Theirs</u> uses pictures to represent words and phrases.

14. Song says she based <u>hers</u> alphabet on Egyptian hieroglyphics.

15. She thinks <u>her</u> is more attractive than mine.

16. George and I used <u>mine</u> computer to develop our code.

Show, Don't Tell

When you describe something, **show, don't tell**, your readers what you mean. You might be describing an old house, a new puppy, or stage fright. In each case, showing is more effective than telling.

Tell That house is old.
Show The house's paint is peeling, and its roof is full of huge holes.

Tell My puppy is cute.
Show My puppy yaps and wags her tail.

Tell I was scared.
Show My tongue dried up, and my knees began to knock uncontrollably.

Rewrite the numbered sentences so that they show rather than tell what the writer means.

The big report was due tomorrow, and I couldn't settle down to work. **(1)** My little brother was noisy. **(2)** The room was messy. **(3)** I was tired. **(4)** Some notes were missing. Suddenly, my mom knocked on the door. "Look outside," she said.

(5) It was snowing.

"There's no school tomorrow," she said.

(6) I was happy.

Imagine that you are in a strange place, such as a desert, a jungle, or a Pharaoh's tomb. Describe what you see, feel, hear, touch, and smell.

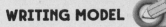

Feature Story

> A **feature story** tells about something that is current and interesting to your readers. The topic may be an event in your town or school or a person that you think your readers would like to know more about. A feature story is factual, but the writing is friendly—and never boring!

Opening clearly introduces topic.

Writer gives necessary background information.

Details help show, not tell, how Ms. Kim felt.

Quotations make writing interesting.

Meet Ms. Kim

Have you noticed the woman who is always smiling outside Room 3? That's Ms. Kim, our school's new second-grade teacher.

Ms. Kim came from Korea to live in this country seventeen years ago.

"I couldn't speak a word of English, and I was afraid of everything," Ms. Kim told me.

"On the first day of school I just stood in a corner and clutched my lunch box tightly."

She still remembers what happened next.

"My teacher's name was Ms. Gleason. She took my hand and showed me my seat. And she was smiling all the time. That's when I knew I had to become a teacher."

So when you see Ms. Kim, say hello to her. And don't forget to smile!

Contractions and Negatives

A **contraction** is a shortened form of two words. An apostrophe takes the place of one or more letters. Some common contractions are given in the table below. Note the spellings of the contractions for *will not (won't)* and *cannot (can't)*.

Contractions with Pronouns and Verbs				Contractions with Verbs and *not*	
I am	I'm	she will	she'll	is not	isn't
he is (has)	he's	you will	you'll	are not	aren't
it is (has)	it's	they will	they'll	was not	wasn't
you are	you're	I had (would)	I'd	were not	weren't
we are	we're	he had (would)	he'd	have not	haven't
they are	they're	she had (would)	she'd	did not	didn't
I have	I've	you had (would)	you'd	does not	doesn't
you have	you've			will not	won't
we have	we've			would not	wouldn't
I will	I'll			should not	shouldn't
he will	he'll			cannot	can't

A Write the contraction for each pair of words.

1. is not

2. they had

3. it is

4. will not

5. she will

6. I have

7. would not

8. did not

9. we are

10. he would

11. have not

12. they are

13. he has

14. was not

15. I am

B Find the word or words in each sentence that can be written as a contraction. Write the word or words and their contraction.

1. I normally do not believe what fortune cookies tell me.
2. This one said, "You will have a surprise today."
3. It did not say what kind of surprise.
4. That morning Mom said she could not drive me to school.
5. I was not happy about this.
6. I had been walking for a few minutes when I saw a sign.
7. "We have got a kitten for you!" the sign said.
8. The man told me he would be happy to give me a kitten.
9. It is only four weeks old.
10. I have never been so excited.
11. I cannot believe my good luck.
12. I will take my fortune cookies more seriously in the future.

C Add a contraction to complete each sentence.

13. "I keep falling off this bike. I ___ ride it," my little sister said.
14. "___ doing great. Just keep pedaling!" we shouted.
15. ___ been trying to ride a bicycle all morning.
16. We thought that maybe ___ learn.
17. "Maybe she ___ old enough," my mom said.
18. Then my sister shouted, "___ riding all by myself!"
19. "___ really easy!" she said.
20. She ___ been off the bike since then.

Test Preparation

 Write the letter of the contraction that correctly completes each sentence.

1. This ___ be an easy crime to solve.

   A isn't   **C** willn't
   B won't   **D** wont

2. The criminal ___ leave any fingerprints.

   A didn't   **C** aren't
   B didnt   **D** didnt'

3. ___ planned this robbery well.

   A Hed'   **C** He'd
   B Heed   **D** H'ed

4. There ___ even any suspects.

   A werent   **C** she's
   B aren't   **D** are'nt

5. Our one witness said she ___ identify the burglar.

   A couldn't   **C** couldnt
   B could'nt   **D** couldnt'

6. We know only that ___ short.

   A its   **C** hes
   B he's   **D** its'

7. ___ be working on this case full-time.

   A Ill   **C** Ile
   B Il'l   **D** I'll

8. ___ going to be a long week.

   A Itz   **C** Its'
   B It's   **D** Its

Review

✓ If the underlined contraction is correct, write *C*. If it is incorrect, write it correctly.

1. My dad <u>does'nt</u> go anywhere without a book.
2. <u>Hes</u> always reading detective stories.
3. If <u>its'</u> about a crime, my dad will read it.
4. Sometimes he <u>cann't</u> put a book down.
5. <u>You'll</u> see him reading in the hall or on the stairs.
6. He <u>willn't</u> go on a trip without a bag full of books.
7. My mom says <u>she'd</u> like Dad to read less.
8. She tells him he <u>isn't</u> any fun with his nose in a book.
9. Dad promises that <u>he'l</u> take a vacation from reading.
10. He <u>has'nt</u> managed to take that vacation yet!

✓ Find two words in each sentence that can be written as a contraction. Write the two words and their contraction.

11. I am solving the mystery of the disappearing cookies.
12. Mom said she would pay me a dollar if I found the thief.
13. She says she does not want a cookie thief in the house.
14. If the cookies continue to vanish, we will not have any left.
15. At first I could not find any clues.
16. Then I thought I would look upstairs.
17. It is strange, but the thief had been in my bedroom.
18. He had left a trail of cookie crumbs on the floor.
19. That did not make sense to me.
20. I have got to get to the bottom of this mystery.

Eliminate Wordiness

Contractions are one way to **eliminate wordiness.** Another way is to drop awkward phrases or replace them with a word or two (*sadly* for *with great sadness; red* for *red in color; if* for *in the event that; because* for *due to the fact that, the reason was because,* or *on account of*).

Wordy	<u>The reason he was puzzled was because</u> he <u>could not</u> solve the case.
Improved	He was puzzled because he couldn't solve the case.
Wordy	Encyclopedia Brown solved the case <u>with great cleverness.</u>
Improved	Encyclopedia Brown cleverly solved the case.

 Improve the sentences by making the underlined phrases less wordy. Rewrite each sentence.

1. Ed looked up at the sky, <u>which was gray in color.</u>

2. He thought it might snow <u>on account of the fact</u> it was so cold.

3. <u>In the event that</u> the weather is bad, I'll stay here.

4. Ed grinned <u>with a lot of cheerfulness</u> and ran home.

 Write an e-mail of three or four sentences to a friend, explaining why he or she should read a favorite book or story. Avoid wordiness.

Writing for Tests

Prompt Write a <u>brief plot summary</u> of <u>a book or movie</u> that you have enjoyed. Tell a friend what happens in the book or movie. Include the <u>important details</u> in the summary. <u>Leave out unnecessary information</u>.

Encyclopedia Brown

Introduction briefly describes the problem.

Chief of Police Brown has a problem. He's expected to solve crimes, but this one has him stumped. Who has stolen the valuable tiger salamander from the Idaville Aquarium?

Writer uses one verb tense (present).

Chief Brown turns to his brainy son Leroy—known as Encyclopedia—for help. Encyclopedia listens to his father's descriptions of the three suspects. One of them is a man named Sam Maine. Sam has only recently been hired, but he claims to have been "taking care of salamanders and other lizards for more than nineteen years."

Summary quotes directly from story to give an important clue.

This statement makes Encyclopedia suspicious. If Sam really knew his salamanders, he wouldn't have said they were lizards. Salamanders are not lizards! If Sam can lie about a former job, he can lie about the crime.

Solution includes only necessary information.

As usual, Encyclopedia Brown has the answer.

Adjectives and Articles

An **adjective** is a word that describes a noun or pronoun. An adjective usually comes before the word it describes, but it can also follow the noun or pronoun. Many adjectives answer the question *What kind?* Others answer *How many?* or *Which one?*

What Kind?	The ship made a <u>cozy</u> home.
How Many?	The *John Ena* had <u>four</u> masts.
Which One?	Classes are held in <u>this</u> room.

A, *an*, and *the* are special adjectives called **articles**. *A* and *an* are used only with singular nouns. Use *the* with both singular and plural nouns.

I had <u>an</u> egg and <u>a</u> slice of toast for breakfast.
<u>The</u> hen laid <u>the</u> eggs.

• Proper adjectives are formed from proper nouns.

Proper Nouns	America, Greece, China
Proper Adjectives	American, Greek, Chinese

A Decide what kind of question each underlined adjective answers. Write *What kind? How many?* or *Which one?*

1. The family lived on a <u>big</u> ship.

2. <u>This</u> ship was called the *John Ena*.

3. The *John Ena* sailed to <u>many</u> parts of the world.

4. The family had many <u>exciting</u> adventures.

5. <u>Several</u> animals lived onboard.

Each sentence contains an adjective and an article. Write the sentence. Underline the adjective. Circle the article.

1. I had a wonderful dream.
2. I was traveling in an enormous balloon.
3. The balloon was lighter than air.
4. It had red letters on the side.
5. I sailed two miles above the ground.
6. A tiny truck raced by below me.
7. Several times the balloon dipped dangerously.
8. It brushed the tops of tall trees.
9. I wasn't nervous for an instant.
10. Now I want to travel in a real balloon.

C Complete the paragraph with adjectives of your own.

(11) My dad took me on a(n) ___ camping trip last summer. (12) We went to some really ___ mountains in New England. (13) ___ mountains are famous for hiking and winter sports. (14) It took about ___ hours to get to the campsite. (15) That first night I went straight to bed because I was ___. (16) The next morning Dad woke me up with a ___ bowl of oatmeal. (17) "We've got ___ miles to cover before sunset," he said. (18) "This is going to be a(n) ___ day." (19) For the next five days, we hiked through ___ forests. (20) We waded across rivers and scrambled up ___ trails. (21) From the tops of mountains we had ___ views. (22) This was the ___ vacation I've ever had.

Test Preparation

Write the letter of the adjective or article in each sentence.

1. Dan lives on an island.

   A island   C lives

   B an   D on

2. This island is a beautiful place.

   A place   C island

   B is   D This

3. It lies five miles off the coast.

   A lies   C coast

   B It   D five

4. The ground is rough and rocky.

   A rocky   C ground

   B and   D is

5. Dan's little house stands right in the middle.

   A stands   C middle

   B little   D in

6. It is made of wood and is painted white.

   A white   C made

   B wood   D painted

7. The windows drip with salty spray.

   A with   C The

   B windows   D drip

8. On stormy days the family stays indoors.

   A family   C days

   B stormy   D stays

Review

✓ Each sentence contains two adjectives. One is underlined. Write the other adjective. (Remember that articles count as adjectives.)

1. We drove across <u>the</u> country in a van.
2. This trip was not <u>easy</u>.
3. Dad and Mom sat in <u>the</u> front seat.
4. Little Jackie and I opened <u>every</u> window.
5. We were often <u>hot</u> and uncomfortable.
6. Ralph, our <u>big</u> yellow dog, was with us too.
7. In Kansas, we heard <u>a</u> loud bang.
8. An <u>engine</u> part had broken.
9. We waited for help for six <u>long</u> hours.
10. We also had two <u>flat</u> tires.
11. Ralph was <u>sick</u>, so we took him to the vet.
12. Mom says smart families take <u>the</u> train.

✓ Write the adjectives in each sentence. The number in ( ) tells how many adjectives are in the sentence. (Do not include articles.)

13. One day last spring, Hilary and I borrowed an old canoe. (3)
14. We weren't expert paddlers, but we expected an easy ride down the river. (2)
15. Ten minutes into the ride, Hilary spotted several silvery fish and leaned over the side. (3)
16. The canoe suddenly tipped and plunged us into the icy water. (1)

Support Your Opinion

When you state an opinion in writing, make sure to **support your opinion** with reasons.

Opinion	Everyone should try sports.
Support	Regular exercise is good for us. We learn to work with others.

Write the number of any sentence that supports the opinion stated in sentence 1.

(1) The *John Ena* was a great place to grow up. **(2)** This four-masted sailing ship was over 300 feet long and 48 feet wide. **(3)** The children had loads of games to play and made friends with members of the crew. **(4)** Just sailing from port to port was a geography lesson in itself. **(5)** The children also got to learn about navigation and the stars from their father. **(6)** They did not enjoy going to school on land. **(7)** There was plenty of fresh air and good food on the *John Ena*. **(8)** Of course, some people got really seasick in rough weather. **(9)** And once a favorite pig fell into a bucket of hot tar. **(10)** The family had wonderful opportunities for fun and learning aboard the *John Ena*.

Each statement below gives an opinion. Write three supporting reasons for each opinion.

11. Summer is better than winter.

12. It is important to go to school.

Book or Story Review

A **book or story review** describes a book or story and gives an opinion about it. A good reviewer includes interesting details about the book and always supports his or her opinion with reasons.

A Home on the Ocean

Catchy opening identifies title and author.

Imagine that your home is in a different place every day. That's what life was like for a girl called Matilda and her brothers and sisters on the *John Ena*. You can read about this lucky family in *Sailing Home: A Story of a Childhood at Sea* by Gloria Rand.

Reviewer gives key background information.

The *John Ena* was a big sailing ship. Matilda's father was the captain, and he took his wife and children with him on his journey. The kids had a great time.

Review includes interesting information from book.

They had many animals and visited dozens of countries. Life wasn't all rosy, though. Sometimes the weather turned ugly, and the children attended school six days a week!

Reviewer gives an opinion and supports it with reasons.

I really enjoyed this book. It made me think about how families live, and it made me want to travel. When you read a book like this, you realize how exciting life can be.

Comparative and Superlative Adjectives

A **comparative adjective** compares two people, places, things, or groups. Add -er to most short adjectives to make their comparative forms. Use *more* with longer adjectives.

- This mountain is <u>taller</u> and <u>more beautiful</u> than that one.

A **superlative adjective** compares three or more people, places, things, or groups. Add -est to most short adjectives to make their superlative forms. Use *most* with longer adjectives.

- It was the <u>highest</u> and <u>most amazing</u> city he had ever seen.

An adjective may change its spelling.

- For adjectives that end with a consonant and *y*, change the *y* to *i* before adding -er or -est: *happy, happier, happiest.*
- For adjectives that end in a single consonant after a single vowel, double the final consonant before adding -er or -est: *big, bigger, biggest.*
- For adjectives that end in *e*, drop the *e* before adding -er or -est: *tame, tamer, tamest.*
- Some adjectives have irregular comparative and superlative forms: *good, better, best; bad, worse, worst.*

A Write the correct form of the adjective in ( ).

   1. This hike is (hard) than the one we took yesterday.

   2. I'm feeling (bad) than I did this morning.

   3. You get the (good) view of all from this cliff.

   4. That is the (remarkable) ruin I have ever seen.

B Change the underlined adjective to the kind of adjective in ( ). Write the new sentence.

1. This was the <u>difficult</u> trip we'd ever taken. (superlative)
2. We saw the <u>fat</u> bugs in the world. (superlative)
3. The snakes were the <u>ferocious</u> ones we'd met. (superlative)
4. It was <u>confusing</u> than the Amazon Basin. (comparative)
5. We took the <u>long</u> time to reach the slopes. (superlative)
6. The mountains were <u>steep</u> than the Andes. (comparative)
7. The weather was <u>snowy</u> than in the Rockies. (comparative)
8. But things could have been <u>bad</u>. (comparative)
9. The views were <u>fine</u> than I'd expected. (comparative)
10. I took the <u>beautiful</u> photographs ever. (superlative)

C Complete the paragraph with adjectives from the box. Put them in comparative or superlative form as necessary. Use each adjective only once.

big	easy	happy	long	tough	uneven

(11) What is the ___ distance you've ever walked? (12) The ___ hike I ever took was the day my brother and I got lost. (13) We were out walking when he said that it would be ___ to take a shortcut than to continue on the trail. (14) Listening to him was the ___ mistake I ever made. (15) We struggled for hours over the ___ country you could imagine. (16) I've never been ___ than when I saw our family car.

Test Preparation

 Write the letter of the word or words that complete each sentence.

1. This is the ___ river in the entire state.

    A most wildest

    B wilder

    C wilderest

    D wildest

2. The water runs ___ here than in the Colorado River.

    A fastest

    B more fast

    C faster

    D most fast

3. It's the ___ place I know for kayaking.

    A better

    B best

    C goodest

    D bestest

4. I guarantee you the ___ ride of your life.

    A excitingest

    B more exciting

    C excitinger

    D most exciting

5. It's ___ in the south than in the north.

    A rockier

    B rockiest

    C rockyer

    D rockyest

Review

✓ If the underlined comparative or superlative adjective is correct, write *C*. If it is incorrect, write it correctly.

1. My friend Ben has <u>better</u> camping equipment than I do.

2. His hiking boots are <u>newest</u> than mine.

3. His backpack is <u>most expensiver</u> than mine.

4. He must have the <u>lighter</u> tent in the world.

5. My camp stove is <u>heavyer</u> than Ben's.

6. His sunglasses have the <u>thinest</u> lenses I've ever seen.

7. His compass is <u>more efficient</u> than my compass.

8. His water filter is the <u>better</u> one money can buy.

9. He has a <u>latest</u> model camera than I do.

10. Ben always carries the <u>advancedest</u> gadgets.

11. But Ben is <u>worser</u> than I am in one area.

12. He is the <u>slowest</u> walker I've ever seen!

✓ Choose the correct form of the adjective in ( ) to complete each sentence. Write the adjective.

13. Are the Andes mountains (good) than the Appalachians?

14. The Appalachians are among the world's (old) mountains.

15. The Andes are (spectacular) than the Appalachians.

16. They are also (difficult) to climb.

17. The Andes are much (high) than the Appalachians.

18. I have seen some of the (red) sunsets ever from their peaks.

19. The Appalachians are (rounded) than the Andes.

20. They also have a (peaceful) appearance.

Choosing Exact Words

Good writers **choose exact words.** Strong verbs, precise nouns, and vivid adjectives make writing clear and lively.

Weak	We <u>went</u> up the steep hill.
Strong	We <u>struggled</u> up the steep hill.
Weak	From the <u>top</u>, we saw a <u>nice</u> sunrise.
Strong	From the <u>rocky summit</u>, we saw a <u>dazzling</u> sunrise.

Replace the underlined word or words with a word or words from the box.

chocolate	disastrous	gasped	hacked
stumbled	tangled vines	scraped	devoured

   Climbing the mountain was easy, but descending was **(1)** <u>very bad</u>. Jules and I **(2)** <u>made</u> a trail through thick bushes all morning. We tripped over **(3)** <u>things</u>. Sharp thorns **(4)** <u>hurt</u> our arms. At noon we **(5)** <u>ate</u> the last of our **(6)** <u>food</u>.

   "I don't think we'll make it," Jules **(7)** <u>said</u>.

   It was dark when we finally **(8)** <u>came</u> out of the forest.

Write a paragraph about a great place to visit. Use exact words to describe the place and make people want to go there.

Editorial

An **editorial** gives an opinion about a current issue. The writer of an editorial speaks directly to the reader and uses exact words and persuasive reasons to support his or her opinion.

Letter to the Editor

Dear Editor:

Opening paragraph summarizes the situation.

> For many years fourth graders at the King School have spent a day at the International Fair in Springfield. This year, Principal Wright has canceled the trip. He argued that students would learn more in class. We think Principal Wright is wrong.

Writer states opinion and supports it with reasons.

Exact words strengthen the argument.

> In school we learn about long division and comparative adjectives. These are useful skills, but there is more to learning than memorizing facts. At the International Fair, students experience how people from other cultures live, dress, eat, and have fun. Students can line dance, make noodles, or practice writing in Arabic.

Writer sums up opinion in conclusion.

> Are we going to lose this opportunity so we can fill out more worksheets? Learning about life is part of our education too!

Ms. Lopez's fourth-grade class

Adverbs

An **adverb** is a word that tells how, when, or where something happens. Adverbs tell about verbs. Adverbs can appear before or after verbs. Many adverbs that tell how something is done end in -*ly*.

How   The plane's engines started <u>noisily</u>. We <u>excitedly</u> watched the takeoff.

When   Our flight leaves <u>soon</u>. We will return <u>later</u>.

Where   I looked <u>around</u>. Were you waiting <u>outside</u>?

A Write the adverb in each sentence.

1. Small planes often use this airport.
2. They taxi slowly along the runway.
3. They rise gracefully into the air.
4. I watch their departure eagerly.
5. I never tire of watching them.

Write *how* if the underlined adverb tells how an action happens. Write *when* if it tells when an action happens. Write *where* if it tells where an action happens.

6. Eleanor Roosevelt <u>sometimes</u> invited Amelia Earhart to the White House.
7. <u>Once</u> the two of them did a surprising thing.
8. They drove <u>quickly</u> to the airport.
9. <u>There</u> they jumped into a plane.
10. They didn't go <u>anywhere</u> in particular.

B Write the adverb in each sentence. Write *how, when,* or *where* to describe what the adverb tells.

1. A funny thing happened yesterday.
2. I woke up early.
3. I went to the window and looked down.
4. Outside in the backyard was a spacecraft.
5. A green creature emerged slowly from the hatch.
6. It pointed a strange machine directly at me.
7. I was floating upward.
8. Then I was in the spacecraft.
9. We flew rapidly through the solar system.
10. Everywhere I looked I could see stars and planets.
11. Finally, the spacecraft returned me to Earth.
12. I floated silently into my bedroom.
13. Suddenly, my mom was calling me for breakfast.
14. I hope I have another dream like that tomorrow.

C Write five sentences of your own using the verbs and adverbs in the box.

Verbs		Adverbs	
fly	travel	rarely	often
go	look	anywhere	down
move		rapidly	

Test Preparation

 Write the letter of the word that is an adverb.

1. We often fly from Midway Airport.

   A fly   **C** often

   B from   **D** Airport

2. We leave early in the morning.

   A morning **C** in

   B leave   **D** early

3. People are coming and going everywhere.

   A everywhere

   B going

   C People

   D are

4. You must wait patiently in line.

   A patiently **C** must

   B line   **D** wait

5. An official will check your bags carefully.

   A official   **C** will

   B carefully **D** check

6. Finally, you can board the plane.

   A get   **C** Finally

   B board   **D** plane

7. I always sit in a window seat.

   A always   **C** seat

   B window **D** sit

8. The plane's engines vibrate noisily.

   A vibrate   **C** plane's

   B engines **D** noisily

Review

✓ Write the adverb in each sentence. One sentence has two adverbs.

1. Wait at the tracks, and look carefully.
2. These trains move quickly.
3. Often the engineer blows a whistle.
4. Express trains never stop at our station.
5. The commuter trains travel slowly.
6. People are standing outside on the platform.
7. Their train will be arriving soon.
8. Yesterday a train derailed.
9. Many of the passengers arrived late to work.
10. Some of them complained angrily about the service.
11. The trains are running smoothly today.
12. People will arrive at their jobs early.

✓ Write the adverb in each sentence. Write *how, when,* or *where* to describe what the adverb tells.

13. My friends wait anxiously for driving lessons.
14. But I travel happily on my bicycle.
15. On my bike I can ride outside in the fresh air.
16. Sometimes I race the squirrels and rabbits.
17. Yesterday I went for a ride on the bike path.
18. I pedaled hard for five miles.

Focus

> Good writers **focus** on the point they want to make. The first sentence of a paragraph generally introduces the topic. All the details and supporting evidence that follow should focus on that topic. Writing without focus can confuse the reader.
>
> | | |
> |---|---|
> | **Topic** | Thomas Edison loved to read. |
> | **On Focus** | He borrowed hundreds of books from the Detroit library. |
> | **Off Focus** | Edison was interested in the telegraph. |

Find the two sentences that do not focus on the main idea of the paragraph. Write the sentences and explain why they do not fit.

Air travel has come a long way since its early days. The very first passengers were in for an adventure. They would sit behind the pilot in an open cockpit. The roar of the engines and the wind whipping past made air travel an exciting experience. Amelia Earhart was one of the first great female pilots. Airlines later added more seats and protection from the weather, but for years flying was far from relaxing. Nowadays, though, air passengers expect high speeds, comfortable seating, and movies. As a result, fewer people travel by train. Travel by airplane today is less adventurous but certainly more convenient!

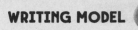

Interview

An **interview** is a special type of conversation between two people. One person—the interviewer—asks questions to learn about the other person—the interviewee. An interviewer should prepare questions that will result in interesting, informative answers.

My Interview with Thomas Edison

Interviewee is introduced to the audience.

Me: Mr. Edison, you are famous as the inventor of the light bulb and sound recording. How did you get started?

Edison: Well, I guess you could say I was a self-starter. You see, I didn't go to school much. My teachers thought I was a slow learner, so my mother let me study at home.

Questions are brief and focused.

Me: What did you study?

Edison: Just about everything. I loved to read fiction and history, but science was my favorite subject. I had a chemistry lab in the basement.

Me: How did your mom feel about that?

Edison: Well, she didn't like the smell, but she was happy that I was learning.

Interview ends with summing up question and answer.

Me: What advice would you give to kids in school today?

Edison: Find something that interests you and learn all you can. Learning is the most exciting thing that a person can do.

Comparative and Superlative Adverbs

A **comparative adverb** compares two actions. Add *-er* to many adverbs to make them comparative. Use *more* with most adverbs that end in *-ly*. Do not use *more* with the *-er* form of an adverb.

> The sun rose <u>later</u> today than it did yesterday, but it shone <u>more brightly</u>.

A **superlative adverb** compares three or more actions. Add *-est* to many adverbs to make them superlative. Use *most* with most adverbs that end in *-ly*. Do not use *most* with an *-est* form.

> Penguins swim <u>fastest</u> and <u>most gracefully</u> of all birds.

Some adverbs, including *well* and *badly*, have irregular comparative and superlative forms: *well, better, best; badly, worse, worst.*

A Write the correct form of the adverb in ( ) to complete each sentence.

1. A whale can dive (more deep, deeper) than a seal.
2. Penguins walk (most slowly, more slowly) than we do.
3. We left early, but we arrived (soonest, sooner) of all.
4. On the last night, the snow fell (most heavily, more heavily) of all.
5. The boat's engine ran (better, best) today than it did yesterday.

B Write the correct form of the adverb in ( ) to complete each sentence. Write *comparative* or *superlative* to identify the adverb you have written.

1. My friend Bob is good at sports, but he does (badly) in school than I do.
2. He can ski (gracefully) than I can.
3. I solve math problems (easily) than Bob does.
4. Bob hits a baseball (hard) of anyone on our team.
5. I scored (high) of all the students on the state English test.
6. Of all the members of the track team, Bob runs (fast).
7. Bob is helping me at basketball so that I'll be able to shoot (accurately) than I do now.
8. I'm helping Bob with English so he'll be able to write (fluently) than he does now.
9. One day I hope to swim (powerfully) than Bob.
10. Bob claims he'll do (well) than me in schoolwork!

C Complete the paragraph below using adverbs from the box. Write the comparative or superlative form.

carefully	fast	fiercely	warmly

(11) If you are not properly dressed, the wind in Antarctica will turn you into a block of ice ____ than you can say, "It's cold out!" (12) Of all the places on Earth, the wind blows ____ there. (13) When I go to Antarctica, I'm going to dress much ____ than I do at home. (14) I will prepare ____ for this expedition than for my earlier trips.

Test Preparation

 Write the letter of the word or words that complete each sentence.

1. The wind blew ____ today than yesterday.

   A gentlyer
   B more gently
   C more gentler
   D most gently

2. The sun shone ____ than it had for days.

   A more brightly
   B most brightly
   C more brightlyer
   D most brightlyer

3. I was able to dress ____ for this hike than for yesterday's.

   A comfortabliest
   B more comfortabler
   C more comfortably
   D most comfortablest

4. Of all the birds, the falcon flies ____ .

   A fastest
   B more faster
   C most fastest
   D fastly

5. It swoops on its prey ____ of the hawks.

   A rapidliest
   B most rapidly
   C rapidest
   D more rapidly

6. The crows caw ____ of all when they see a falcon.

   A noisyest
   B most noisily
   C more noisily
   D more noisiest

Review

✓ Write the correct form of the adverb in ( ) to complete each sentence.

1. In March the sun shines (more stronger, more strongly) than in February.

2. The days last (longer, more longer) than in deep winter.

3. Rivers run (more rapidly, most rapidest) than in January.

4. Of all locations, snow clings (most stubbornly, more stubborner) to the high ground.

5. On the mountains, the temperature drops (most sharpest, most sharply) than anywhere else.

6. Of all the months, the wind blows (worse, worst) in March.

✓ Write the comparative or superlative form of the adverb in ( ) to complete each sentence.

(7) Out of all the Midwestern states, I vacation (frequently) in Michigan. (8) For me, the breeze blows (freshly) there than in Wisconsin. (9) I know it's not really true, but the sun seems to shine (brilliantly) in Michigan than in Indiana. (10) I can't think of another place where the fish jump (high). (11) Of all the places I've traveled, I think of Michigan (fondly). (12) I hope to go to Michigan (often) next year than I have in the past.

Know Your Audience

Before you write, take a moment to think about your readers. When you **know your audience**, you can choose the right words, details, and tone.

To the Editor Many students oppose having classes on Saturdays.

To Your Friends If they think I'm going to school on Saturday, they're crazy!

Write the letter of the sentence that matches each audience.

1. Teacher

  A I hope that you'll feel better soon.

  B Hurry up and get better, dude.

2. Classmate

  A Hey, how's it going?

  B I wish you a good day.

3. Newspaper Reader

  A The food here really stinks.

  B Food in the cafeteria could be much better.

Write the first two sentences in a letter of acceptance to the group below, accepting what is described.

To: the school Parents' Association; *What:* reading award

Letter of Acceptance

A **letter of acceptance** is a response to an offer of a job or another opportunity. This type of letter should be brief, respectful, and written in formal English.

A Cook for Columbus

July 1492

Dear Captain Columbus:

Opening comes to the point immediately.

I am delighted that you have agreed to employ me as a cook on your Atlantic voyage. I accept with pleasure.

Formal English is used to address someone who is not a close friend.

As I told you in my interview, I have never believed that the Earth is flat. It is exciting to be setting out on a trip to prove that people can reach the East by sailing west.

Writer requests further information.

I do have one further question. Some people say that there are other lands between here and India. This sounds unlikely, but it would allow us to stock up on fresh fruit and meat during the voyage. What is your opinion?

Closing sentence returns to main idea.

I am honored to be sailing with you next month.

Yours truly,
Pablo Vasquez

Prepositions and Prepositional Phrases

A **preposition** begins a group of words called a **prepositional phrase**. A prepositional phrase ends with a noun or pronoun called the **object of the preposition**. The preposition shows how the object of the preposition is related to other words in the sentence. A prepositional phrase can be used to tell *where, when, how,* or *which one*.

Preposition   The boys walked <u>on</u> the rough ground.

Prepositional Phrase   <u>on the rough ground</u>

Object of the Preposition   <u>ground</u>

Common Prepositions
about, above, across, after, along, around, at, behind, below, beneath, between, by, for, from, in, into, of, on, over, through, to, under, upon, with, without

A Write the prepositional phrase in each sentence. Underline the preposition. Circle the object of the preposition.

1. Vern and Gerry left their shelter at night.
2. The boys jumped over gullies.
3. Vern fell into a deep crack.
4. He landed on his leg.
5. The power in Vern's suit stopped working.
6. Gerry helped Vern back to the shelter.

B Each sentence below contains two prepositional phrases. Write the prepositional phrases.

1. Let's go around the galaxy in my spaceship.
2. My ship is powered with energy from the sun.
3. It travels at the speed of light.
4. A famous inventor gave it to me for my birthday.
5. It was made by robots at his factory.
6. The passenger sits behind the pilot in the cockpit.
7. You can look at the stars through the windows.
8. We could zoom across the solar system and coast over the Milky Way.
9. Between Jupiter and Saturn we could stop for lunch.
10. After lunch we could play on Saturn's rings.
11. With this spaceship you should have no worries about anything.
12. We'll be back in time for tomorrow's classes!

C Add a prepositional phrase of your own to each sentence. Write the new sentences.

13. There are trillions of stars ____ .
14. Doria enjoys watching the stars ____ .
15. She watches them ____ .
16. She sets up a telescope ____ .
17. Doria has a book ____ .
18. She wants to study astronomy ____ .
19. Astronomy is the study ____ .
20. One day Doria might travel ____ .

Test Preparation

✓ Write the letter of the word that is a preposition.

1. The sky is full of shooting stars.

   A sky   C stars
   B full   D of

2. We have watched them for many hours.

   A many   C for
   B them   D hours

3. The meteors streak through the sky.

   A through
   B streak
   C meteors
   D sky

4. They burn up upon contact with Earth's atmosphere.

   A burn
   B Earth's
   C upon
   D atmosphere

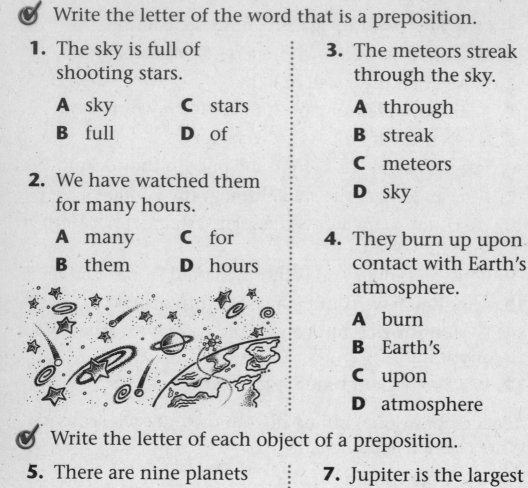

✓ Write the letter of each object of a preposition.

5. There are nine planets in the solar system.

   A There   C in
   B system   D planets

6. All the planets go around the sun.

   A around   C sun
   B planets   D all

7. Jupiter is the largest of these planets.

   A these   C largest
   B Jupiter   D planets

8. Pluto is the planet farthest from our Earth.

   A our   C Pluto
   B farthest   D Earth

Review

✓ Write the prepositional phrase in each sentence.

1. Is there intelligent life on other planets?
2. For centuries, people have been asking this question.
3. So far, however, we are without an answer.
4. Astronomers haven't even found another planet with a suitable atmosphere.
5. If such a planet exists, it is probably far from our solar system.
6. In another fifty years, maybe we will have an answer.

✓ Write the prepositional phrase in each sentence. Underline the preposition. Circle the object of the preposition.

7. When I was five, I built a rocket ship in my basement.
8. It was made from cardboard.
9. My big brother helped me with the construction.
10. I believed that this rocket ship would take me to the moon.
11. I thought the moon was just above our house.
12. On a fine Thursday evening, I was ready.
13. The rocket ship was on its launch pad.
14. I climbed into the cockpit.
15. I was all prepared for my long trip.
16. For several minutes I sat and waited.
17. After a long time I got out.
18. The failure of my ship puzzled me.

WRITER'S CRAFT

Using Persuasive Words

One way to persuade a reader to agree with you is to use **persuasive words**. Some persuasive words are in favor of something, such as *important, best,* and *great*. Some are against something, such as *awful, worst,* and *terrible*. Words such as *should* and *must* are also persuasive.

You <u>must</u> read this <u>incredible</u> book.

No one <u>should</u> watch that <u>awful</u> show.

Write the persuasive words or phrases that the writer uses in the following paragraph.

I've just seen the most amazing movie. It's called *Journey to the Center of the Earth,* and it was made a long time ago. The plot is very exciting. It's about a scientist who leads a group of people underground through an extinct volcano. They have incredible adventures, including fighting some weird-looking dinosaurs. (The special effects are pretty bad!) The end is thrilling. All the people get shot into the air by a volcano.

Write two persuasive sentences about each subject below.

1. A bad song

2. A good soccer team

3. A terrible TV show

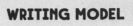

Write Your Opinion

When you **write your opinion**, you tell what you think about a topic. To persuade your readers to agree with you, support your opinion with reasons.

Opening catches reader's interest.

Writer uses persuasive words effectively.

Opinions are supported with reasons.

Conclusion restates main idea.

Amazing Science Fiction

How would you like to go back in time and meet a dinosaur? Would you enjoy a short walk on the planet Mars? Maybe you'd prefer to watch from another galaxy as our Earth explodes!

To the reader of science fiction, these incredible adventures are just a turn of a page away. Science fiction allows us to do the impossible without leaving our armchairs. Reading science fiction is also a great way to learn. How cold is it at night on the moon? Will we ever travel in time? Read science fiction to find out.

Everyone should give science fiction a try. It adds excitement and imagination to our lives.

Conjunctions

Conjunctions are connecting words, such as *and, but,* and *or.* They can be used to join words, phrases, and sentences.

- Use *and* to add information or to join related ideas: They played soccer <u>and</u> tag.
- Use *but* to join different ideas: Some people were kind, <u>but</u> others were mean.
- Use *or* to suggest a choice: We can fight with each other, <u>or</u> we can get along.

Conjunctions make compound subjects, compound predicates, and compound sentences. There is a comma before the conjunction in a compound sentence.

Compound Subject	Christine <u>and</u> M.L. lived in Georgia.
Compound Predicate	They grew up <u>and</u> went to school in Atlanta.
Compound Sentence	The children wanted to play, <u>but</u> their parents wouldn't let them. (Note the comma.)

A Write the conjunction in each sentence.

1. Christine King and her brother were born in Atlanta.

2. The Kings were not wealthy, but they were happy.

3. M.L. vowed to change this injustice, and he did.

4. You can accept life, or you can try to improve things.

B Tell whether each sentence contains a compound subject or a compound predicate. Write *CS* for compound subject and *CP* for compound predicate.

1. Martin Luther King, Jr., and other leaders helped change our country.
2. They spoke against injustice and protested publicly.
3. Officials criticized and imprisoned these people.
4. In the 1960s, blacks and whites marched for civil rights.
5. Violence and arrests often broke up these marches.
6. The protesters never gave in or gave up.
7. They marched and sang and prayed for change.
8. Leaders today study and learn from King's ideas.

C Use the conjunction *and*, *but*, or *or* to join each pair of sentences. Write each new sentence with a comma.

9. Doing the right thing is important. It is often difficult.
10. Do you want to be popular? Will you speak out?
11. You can face reality. You can ignore the truth.
12. Martin Luther King, Jr., always spoke his mind. Not everyone liked his opinions.

Test Preparation

☑ Write the letter of the word that completes each sentence.

1. A small ___ important incident happened in first grade.

   A or   **C** so
   B then   **D** but

2. It was recess, ___ I was on the playground.

   A but   **C** or
   B and   **D** then

3. I was probably playing tag ___ kickball.

   A or   **C** like
   B and   **D** but

4. A fifth-grade boy came up to me ___ grabbed my shirt.

   A but   **C** or
   B and   **D** since

5. "Give me your lunch money, ___ you'll be sorry," he said.

   A and   **C** or
   B if   **D** than

6. I wanted to run, ___ he was holding my shirt tightly.

   A and   **C** or
   B but   **D** when

7. At that moment a little girl named Ada ran up ___ stood between us.

   A or   **C** but
   B then   **D** and

8. Ada was only a year older than me, ___ she was not afraid.

   A and   **C** but
   B so   **D** that

Review

✔ Write the conjunction in ( ) that completes each sentence.

1. My mom (and, but) dad taught me to speak the truth.
2. They gave me good advice, (and, but) it has not always been easy to follow.
3. People don't always agree with you (but, or) want to hear your opinions.
4. Sometimes you should do something, (but, or) you end up doing nothing.
5. I feared losing friends (but, and) sometimes took the easy way out.
6. In fact, people often admire (but, and) follow you for speaking the truth.
7. Your words may change their thoughts (or, but) affect their actions.
8. Speaking your own mind can be frightening, (or, but) it's worth it.

✔ Use the conjunction *and*, *but*, or *or* to join each pair of sentences. Write each new sentence with a comma.

9. Everyone in my family sets personal goals in January. At the end of the year we review them.
10. Our goals are interesting. We don't always achieve them.
11. My big sister wanted to be a star basketball player. She didn't even make the school team.
12. Would you rather set yourself an easy task? Would you prefer an impossible dream?

Sentence Variety

Sentence variety makes writing flow smoothly.

- Include interrogative, exclamatory, and imperative sentences.
- Combine short related sentences, using words such as *but*, *and*, *although*, *because*, and *while*.
- Vary sentence beginnings and lengths.

Without Transitions	I ran fast. I was late.
With Transitions	Although I ran fast, I was late.
Same Beginning	We will win in spring. We will celebrate then.
Different Beginnings	In spring, we will win. Then we will celebrate.

Combine the two short, choppy sentences in each pair. Use the transition word in ( ). Write the new sentence. Remember to add a comma before *and* and *but*.

1. I can't go to school. I'm not feeling well. (because)
2. I tried getting out of bed. I felt dizzy. (but)
3. I'm still sleepy. It's nearly noon. (although)
4. My nose is running. I have a headache. (and)
5. Would you buy cough drops? You go to the store. (if)

Write a description of your favorite food, book, TV show, or sport. Vary sentence types and beginnings.

Biography

A **biography** tells the story of a person's life. Some biographies, like those in books, are long. Others, like the one below, are short. Whatever its length, a biography must include key facts of a person's life and explain why the person is important.

A Man of Peace

Opening sentence clearly introduces subject.

Mohandas Gandhi was not a politician or a general, but he became one of the great leaders of the 20th century.

Gandhi was born in India in 1869. He was a shy boy who did not excel in school, but he cared deeply about the Indian people.

Writer includes important background facts.

In those days Britain ruled India and made its laws. Gandhi wanted his people to be free and to live as equals in a just society. He led his people against the British, using not weapons, but peaceful protests. After more than 30 years of nonviolent struggle, India became a free country.

Varied sentences create smooth style.

Closing sentence summarizes subject's importance.

Gandhi was assassinated in 1948, but his spirit lived on. Far away in America, a young man named Martin Luther King, Jr., read about Gandhi and followed his teachings.

Capitalization

Here are some rules for **capitalizing** proper nouns.

- Capitalize the first word and every important word of a proper noun. Proper nouns name particular persons, places, or things.

    Jim **T**horpe was born in what is now **O**klahoma. His mother was a **N**ative **A**merican. He went to **C**arlisle **I**ndian **S**chool in **P**ennsylvania.

- Capitalize the first letter of an abbreviation. Capitalize both letters in a state postal abbreviation.

    14 **C**olumbus **S**t.   **T**ulsa, **OK**

- Capitalize days of the week, months of the year, and holidays.

    Saturday   **S**eptember   **P**residents' **D**ay

- Capitalize titles that are used before people's names.
    Everyone called **M**r. Warner **C**oach Warner.

A Write *C* if the group of words is capitalized correctly. If the group of words is capitalized incorrectly, rewrite it using correct capitalization.

1. American indian
2. Chief black hawk
3. Mauch Park, PA
4. Haskell institute
5. Saturday afternoon
6. Fourth of July
7. U.S. postal service
8. 47 Jim Thorpe St.
9. Phillips school
10. Appalachian mountains
11. Raleigh, NC
12. dr. Mary Reiter

B Correct the capitalization in each sentence. Write the new paragraph.

(1) every may, fourth-grade students at lincoln elementary school go on a field trip. (2) This generally takes place the week before memorial day. (3) our outing this year is on tuesday, may 26. (4) we are going to visit mt. clement cemetery in centerville. (5) ms. lopez and principal skinner will be leading the trip. (6) we've each been assigned a soldier who died in the civil war. (7) I've been assigned major john peters from maryland. (8) mark petrie and joan lipkis will be working with me. (9) after our visit to the cemetery, we will stop for lunch at a restaurant in niles. (10) then we will report on major peters on thursday at the meeting of the pta.

C Rewrite each sentence. Add the information in ( ). Use correct capitalization.

11. What are you doing on (date and month)?

12. Come with me to the track meet in (city and state).

13. It's at the (center or field).

14. That is part of (school or college).

15. The exact address is (street).

16. I'm taking a bus from (city) to (city).

17. Why don't we meet at (train station)?

18. (teacher) and (coach) will be there too.

Test Preparation

✓ Write the letter of the group of words that is correct.

1. A Madison square garden
   B madison square Garden
   C Madison Square Garden
   D Madison Square garden

2. A New York, NY 10001
   B New York, Ny 10001
   C New york, NY 10001
   D New York, ny 10001

3. A Monday through friday
   B Monday through Friday
   C Monday Through Friday
   D monday through friday

4. A New york Knicks
   B new york Knicks
   C new york knicks
   D New York Knicks

5. A Fourth of July celebration
   B fourth of July Celebration
   C Fourth of july celebration
   D Fourth Of July Celebration

6. A saturday, june 5
   B Saturday, june 5
   C Saturday, June 5
   D Saturday, JUNE 5

7. A 4 Pennsylvania Plaza
   B 4 Pennsylvania plaza
   C 4 pennsylvania plaza
   D 4 pennsylvania Plaza

8. A parker Middle school
   B Parker Middle School
   C Parker middle school
   D parker Middle School

Review

Write *C* if the group of words is capitalized correctly. If the group of words is capitalized incorrectly, rewrite it using correct capitalization.

1. 4475 Colonial ave.
2. Dr. and mrs. William Springer
3. veterans Day
4. South Ellison Medical center
5. open May through September
6. Santa Fe, Nm
7. the third Wednesday of the Month
8. Jefferson Elementary School
9. San Francisco giants
10. Martin Luther King, Jr.

Rewrite the sentences using correct capitalization.

11. tuesday, june 14, is an important day in our school calendar.
12. that's when the fourth-grade students from park ridge primary school will play softball against their teachers and dr. noble.
13. if you want to watch, go to sadler memorial playground at 2 in the afternoon.
14. a reporter from nashville, tennessee, will be writing a story about the game.
15. There is plenty of free parking on tomkins drive.
16. if the students win the game, we will have a party in mid-september, two weeks after labor day.

Paraphrasing

When you take notes on facts in a book or article, you are **paraphrasing**.

- Paraphrase only the main ideas.
- Use your own words and word order, not those of the author.
- Copy especially interesting sentences in quotation marks.

Read the paragraph and each paraphrase of the paragraph. Write the best description from the box for each paraphrase.

Wording too close to original paragraph
Restates important facts in own words

Jim Thorpe was an excellent athlete but not so good a student. Then Jim's mother died, and his father died soon after. Jim was heartbroken but decided to follow his father's advice and stay in school. At a boarding school in Carlisle, Pennsylvania, Coach Pop Warner had Jim try out for the football team, and the boy amazed everyone with his ability.

1. Jim Thorpe had a hard childhood, but he stayed in school and became a star of Coach Pop Warner's football team.

2. Jim Thorpe was an excellent athlete but not so good a student. At boarding school in Pennsylvania, Coach Pop Warner gave Jim a tryout for the football team.

Taking Notes

When you **take notes**, you write down the most important facts in a story or article. You don't have to write complete sentences or spell out all the words. Write the key points briefly and in your own words. You can use your notes to review the facts or to write a complete report. The notes below are from a biography of the football player Jim Thorpe.

Notes are written in list form.

Writer uses abbreviations and does not always use complete sentences.

Order of events is the same as in story.

Writer includes important names and places.

Notes on *Jim Thorpe's Bright Path*

JT born 1887 in log cabin in OK

Mother is Indian—father part Indian

Parents want good education for their boys.

JT goes to Indian boarding schools.

Not a good student but very good at sports

Twin brother dies at school—mom and dad die too.

Starts working hard at school

Goal—to play football

Gets big break at Carlisle Indian School, PA

Sets school record in high jump

Coach Pop Warner gives JT tryout for football team.

JT proves he's a star.

Commas

Here are some rules for using **commas**.

- Use commas to separate items in a series.

    We grew squash, eggplants, and corn.

- Use commas to set off the name of someone being spoken to. This is called *direct address*.

    Miguel, have you watered the garden? Yes, Tía, I have. Have a smoothie, Miguel.

- Use commas after introductory words and phrases.

    Yes, I like a purple house. Of course, it is a little bright.

- Use commas in dates and addresses.

    Between the day and the month: Saturday, June 23

    Between the date and the year: August 14, 2005

    Between the city and the state: Boise, Idaho

A Add one comma to correct each sentence. Write the sentences.

1. Miguel could play shortstop second base, or third base.
2. His big moment happened on Tuesday August 22, 2005.
3. That day he hit a single a double, a triple, and a home run.
4. Pedro Martínez Juan Marichal, and Sammy Sosa are Dominican baseball players.
5. Martínez was born on October 25 1971.
6. He played from 1997 to 2004 in Boston Massachusetts.

B Write the sentences. Add commas as needed.

1. Where were you born Miguel?
2. I was born in Peru on April 23 1998.
3. My goodness that's a long way from Seattle!
4. Well my dad got a job here.
5. I've also lived in Texas Utah and New York.
6. I live with my parents three sisters and a dog.
7. My favorite sports are baseball basketball and soccer.
8. Of course learning English is very important.
9. I want to be a lawyer a musician or a baseball player.
10. We will become U.S. citizens on Monday May 7.
11. There's a special ceremony in Seattle Washington.
12. Believe me we'll be happy to be Americans.
13. We're celebrating with a red white and blue cake!
14. Miguel it's been great talking to you.

C The note below requires twelve commas to punctuate it correctly. Write the note with the added commas.

(15) Monday May 14 2_____

(16) You wouldn't believe the day I've had Maria! (17) Coach made us run ten laps take batting practice field fly balls and play a practice game. (18) Then I had to go with my mom to pick up Dad in Portsmouth New Hampshire. (19) Did I say that I had homework in math English history and Spanish? (20) After all this my good friend I am ready for bed!

Test Preparation

Write the letter of the group of words that is correct.

1. ___ that you played professional baseball?

   A Is it true, Uncle Sal,
   B Is it, true Uncle Sal
   C Is it true, Uncle Sal
   D Is it, true, Uncle Sal

2. ___ in the minors for two seasons.

   A Yes I played,
   B Yes, I played
   C Yes I, played
   D Yes I played

3. My first team was ___.

   A in Akron Ohio
   B in, Akron, Ohio
   C in, Akron Ohio
   D in Akron, Ohio

4. I showed up for practice on ___.

   A March, 1 1997
   B March, 1, 1997
   C March 1, 1997
   D March 1 1997

5. My best game was on ___.

   A Wednesday, July 3
   B Wednesday July 3
   C Wednesday, July, 3
   D Wednesday July, 3

6. I hit a single, ___ and a home run.

   A two, doubles a triple
   B two doubles a triple,
   C two doubles, a triple,
   D two doubles a triple

Review

✓ Write *C* if commas are used correctly. If commas are not used correctly, rewrite the sentences, adding commas as needed.

1. Did you know Ed, that I kept a journal from June 22 to July 31, 2006?
2. That summer we drove from Baltimore to Portland Oregon.
3. Boy that was an amazing trip!
4. My first entry is dated Saturday June 22.
5. That night we stayed with friends in Albany, New York.
6. We saw Ohio, Indiana Illinois, Iowa South Dakota, and many other states.
7. One night we camped near Jackson, Wyoming.
8. Here is the conversation I heard between Lindy and Mom that night Ed.
9. Mom I hear something funny.
10. Just go back to sleep honey.

✓ The paragraph requires eight commas to punctuate it correctly. Write the paragraph with the added commas.

(11) On my calendar I have circled June 24 2008. (12) That's when I'm going to football camp in West Allis Wisconsin. (13) We'll practice blocking running and tackling. (14) Needless to say I'm really excited. (15) We'll play other camps from Minnesota Illinois and Michigan. (16) Camp is over on Sunday July 7.

Good Conclusions

> A strong piece of writing has a **good conclusion.**
> A conclusion may restate the main idea in a new
> way, tell what the writer feels or has learned, or
> pose a question for readers to think about. A good
> conclusion signals that the writing is at an end.

Read the paragraph and the three conclusions.
Write the best description from the box
about each conclusion.

> Restates main idea in a new way
> Tells what the writer feels or has learned
> Poses a question for readers to think about

    Mr. Frazier seems like he hates everyone. He sounds
mean on his answering machine. It's as if he's saying, "Go
away and don't bother me." He spies on his neighbors and
writes them a rude letter. But there's more to Mr. Frazier than
just grumpiness. He freezes his field so neighbor kids can play
hockey there, and he attends their big game.

    1. Why does he do that if he doesn't like people?

    2. Although he may not like people, he loves hockey.

    3. Underneath his gruffness, Mr. Frazier may be a
        lonely boy who just wants to play sports.

Write a paragraph about a real or fictional character.
Add a good conclusion.

Character Sketch

When you write a **character sketch,** you are telling the reader what a story character or real person is like. A character sketch vividly describes the person's actions and character traits.

A Very Colorful Aunt

Writer names character traits.

Tía Lola is an amazing aunt. She's fun, stubborn, and smart. Those stories she tells at night keep everyone up past bedtime. And no one makes better smoothies!

Specific examples support each trait.

Tía Lola can also be difficult at times. She's strong-minded and does what she wants. When she thinks the house would look better purple, she just goes ahead and paints it. This makes life complicated for Mami and her family.

Writer discusses most important trait last.

Here's where another side of Tía Lola comes in. This is a very smart woman! She knows how much grumpy old Colonel Charlebois loves baseball, so she warms his heart with a special baseball party. By the end, even the Colonel likes a purple house!

A lively conclusion wraps up the sketch.

Quotations and Quotation Marks

A speaker's exact words are called a **quotation.** When you write a quotation, put **quotation marks (" ")** at the beginning and end of the speaker's exact words. Begin the quotation with a capital letter.

- If the quotation comes last in a sentence, use a comma to separate it from the rest of the sentence:

  Orville said**,** "We are making a flying machine."

- If the quotation comes first, use a comma, question mark, or exclamation mark to separate it from the rest of the sentence:

  "What a ridiculous idea**!**" a friend remarked.

- Place the end punctuation mark of a quotation before the closing quotation mark:

  "Don't you think we can do it**?**" asked Wilbur.

A If a sentence is written correctly, write C. Three sentences are not written correctly. Add quotation marks and rewrite them.

1. "Let's try bending the wings," Wilbur suggested.

2. Why would we do that? asked Orville.

3. "Then our glider can circle like a bird," said Wilbur.

4. Orville shouted, "What a terrific idea!"

5. "Why were the Wright brothers successful?" I asked.

6. Our teacher paused and said, They tested everything.

B Add quotation marks and rewrite each sentence.

   1. Will asked, Which do you like better, cars or planes?
   2. Anna said, Oh, I like cars much better.
   3. She continued, They're more convenient.
   4. Can you imagine picking up a pizza in a plane? she asked.
   5. I wouldn't want to cross the ocean in a car, laughed Kim.
   6. Anna replied, Try parking a plane in your driveway!
   7. Cars always have accidents, Kim pointed out.
   8. And I've never heard of a plane in a traffic jam, he added.
   9. Can you take me to school in an airplane? Anna asked.
   10. Kim answered, I can if your school has an airport.
   11. This is a silly argument, remarked Sandy.
   12. Cars and planes have different purposes, she said.

C Rewrite each sentence. Add quotation marks and other correct punctuation.

   13. What would be the best invention in the world asked Erica
   14. Ty answered I'd vote for a flying bicycle
   15. What a great idea that is said Erica
   16. How would it work she asked
   17. Ty said thoughtfully well it would be a bike with folding wings
   18. Would the wings flap like a bird's Erica wondered
   19. No you'd take off like a plane explained Ty
   20. Erica laughed I'd love to fly to school.
   21. Let's start making one after school suggested Ty
   22. We'll be millionaires they shouted together

Test Preparation

☑ Write the letter of the answer that completes each sentence correctly.

1. "Will we actually ride in a ___ asked Amy.

   A basket?

   B basket?"

   C basket"

   D "basket?"

2. "That's how balloonists ___ replied Mr. Thorne.

   A travel,

   B travel"

   C travel,"

   D travel."

3. "Are there ___ Tom asked.

   A seats?"

   B seats,"

   C seats!"

   D seats"?

4. Mr. Thorne smiled and said, ___ room only."

   A It's standing"

   B "It's standing,"

   C "it's standing

   D "It's standing

5. "I'll bet there isn't a video ___ complained Tom.

   A either"

   B either

   C either,"

   D either,

6. "I'm ___ Amy.

   A scared?" wailed

   B scared!" wailed

   C scared"! wailed

   D scared wailed,"

7. Mr. Thorne shouted to the ground ___ go of the ropes!"

   A crew! "Let

   B crew," Let

   C crew, "let

   D crew, "Let

8. "We're ___ yelled.

   A off!" he

   B off!" He

   C off" he

   D off! he

Review

✓ Write the sentence in each pair that uses quotation marks correctly.

1. "I will prove that time travel is possible," Jim said.
   "I will prove that time travel is possible, Jim," said.

2. "What is the box for" asked Ray?
   "What is the box for?" asked Ray.

3. Jim looked serious and said, "it's my time machine."
   Jim looked serious and said, "It's my time machine."

4. "That's a washing machine box Liz laughed."
   "That's a washing machine box," Liz laughed.

5. Just watch this, replied Jim, "Stepping into the box."
   "Just watch this," replied Jim, stepping into the box.

6. His classmates gasped, "The box just vanished!"
   His classmates gasped! "The box just vanished".

✓ Rewrite the sentences using quotation marks and other punctuation as needed.

7. When Jim suddenly returned, one classmate said You played a trick on us

8. Show us how you disappeared another demanded

9. I told you it's a time machine Jim replied

10. One boy shouted out Prove it

11. All right Jim answered

12. He continued look at this large round object

13. What's that asked his classmates

14. It's a dinosaur egg announced Jim with a smile

Include Important Details

When you write a research report, use the facts to make an outline. Keep your topic, audience, and purpose in mind. Then **include only important details** about your topic in your report.

Below is part of an outline and two paragraphs based on it. Write the sentences that do not belong in the paragraphs because they contain unimportant details.

B. Propellers
    1. Curved blades better than flat blades
    2. One on each side behind wings
    3. Connected to motor by bicycle chain
C. Engine
    1. Automobile engines too heavy
    2. Wrights design their own engine
    3. Made of lightweight cast aluminum

The Wright brothers learned that curved propeller blades worked better than flat ones. They mounted a propeller on each wing of their Flyer. This was long before the invention of jet engines. Each propeller was connected to the engine with bicycle chain. I have never flown in a plane.

The brothers also discovered that automobile engines were too heavy for flight. Automobiles were old-fashioned looking in those days. Using cast aluminum, they designed their own lightweight aircraft engine for the plane.

Outlining

Make an **outline** to organize important ideas in a piece of writing. Divide the outline into main sections and give each section a title. List key ideas in that section, using letters and numbers to show their importance. Below is part of an outline. A complete outline would have more sections, including a Roman numeral II.

Roman numeral indicates main section.

Main titles use capital letters for key words.

Information is in note form.

Capital letters, numbers, and small letters show ideas in main section.

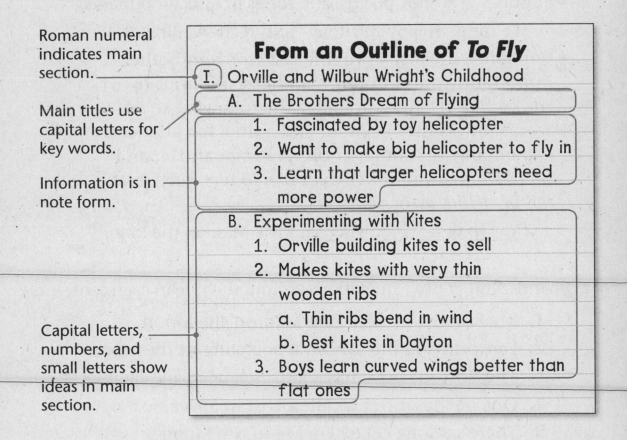

From an Outline of *To Fly*

I. Orville and Wilbur Wright's Childhood

  A. The Brothers Dream of Flying

    1. Fascinated by toy helicopter

    2. Want to make big helicopter to fly in

    3. Learn that larger helicopters need more power

  B. Experimenting with Kites

    1. Orville building kites to sell

    2. Makes kites with very thin wooden ribs

      a. Thin ribs bend in wind

      b. Best kites in Dayton

    3. Boys learn curved wings better than flat ones

Titles

In your writing, underline the **titles** of books, magazines, and newspapers. When these titles appear in printed material, they are set in italic type.

Handwritten the <u>Washington Post</u>, <u>National Geographic</u>, <u>Charlotte's Web</u>

Printed the *Washington Post, National Geographic, Charlotte's Web*

- Put titles of stories, poems, and songs in quotation marks.

    We sang "Happy Birthday" and recited "Birches."

- Capitalize the first word, the last word, and other important words in titles. Capitalize all forms of the verb *be*. Do not capitalize the following short words unless they begin or end a title: the articles *a*, *an*, and *the;* the conjunctions *and*, *but*, and *or*; and prepositions with fewer than five letters, such as *to, for, in, of, on, at,* or *with.*

    <u>How to Be a Star at Baseball</u>, "The Man on the Moon"

A Underline or place quotations around the title in each sentence.

1. My favorite book is First Man on the Moon.

2. Footprints in the Sand is a poem about the moon.

3. The Boston Globe has a kids' science page each week.

4. One of the stories is called Lost in Space.

5. There's a song called Fly Me to the Moon.

6. Do you know the song Fly Away?

B Correct any mistake in capitalization in the title. Write *Correct* if the title has no errors.

1. "Slam, Dunk, And Hook"

2. Rosa Parks: my Story

3. "Oh Broom, Get To Work"

4. "The Courage That My Mother Had"

5. "the Song That Never ends"

6. The Monsters are Due on Maple Street

7. How Night Came From the Sea

8. "I'll Walk the Tightrope"

9. "Cat And Rat: The Legend of The Chinese Zodiac"

10. "There is No Word for Goodbye"

11. "Americans Worry about the Decline of the Oceans"

12. Belmont Citizen and Record

C Find the titles in the following sentences. Then copy the sentences, writing the titles correctly. The words in ( ) tell you what the titles are.

13. The house at pooh corner is about Winnie the Pooh. (book)

14. Does Dad subscribe to modern computers? (magazine)

15. Our class likes to recite casey at the bat. (poem)

16. there was a young fellow of ealing is a funny poem. (poem)

17. The night the bed fell also makes me laugh. (story)

18. My uncle reads the toronto globe and mail. (newspaper)

Test Preparation

✓ Write the letter of the title that completes each sentence correctly.

1. ___ is one of many poems my aunt can recite.

A The Wreck of the Hesperus
B "The Wreck Of the Hesperus"
C "The Wreck of the Hesperus"
D The Wreck of The Hesperus

2. Singing ___ always makes me smile.

A "Happy Days are here Again"
B "Happy days are here Again"
C "Happy Days are Here Again"
D "Happy Days Are Here Again"

3. Chapter 1 of ___ was very exciting.

A "The Wind on the Moon"
B The Wind on the Moon
C "The wind on the Moon"
D The Wind on The Moon

4. ___ is the story we are reading now.

A "Bums in the Attic"
B "Bums in the attic"
C Bums in the Attic
D Bums in the Attic

5. I have to cut out pictures and articles from the ___.

A New york Times
B "New York Times"
C "New York times"
D New York Times

6. There are hundreds of ___ magazines in our basement.

A "Popular Mechanics"
B Popular Mechanics
C "Popular mechanics"
D Popular mechanics

7. Mom's reading a novel called ___.

A "In the Time of the Butterflies"
B "In the time of the Butterflies"
C In the Time of the Butterflies
D In The Time of The Butterflies

Review

✓ Write the sentence in each pair in which the title is written correctly.

1. "Magic Story for Falling Asleep" is a lovely poem.

Magic Story for Falling Asleep is a lovely poem.

2. Mom's favorite song is <u>Swing Low, Sweet Chariot</u>.

Mom's favorite song is "Swing Low, Sweet Chariot."

3. "The Second Tree from the Corner" is a good book.

<u>The Second Tree from the Corner</u> is a good book.

4. <u>Reader's Digest</u>, a small magazine, is easy to carry.

"Reader's Digest," a small magazine, is easy to carry.

5. Dad says "The Pit and the Pendulum" is a scary story.

Dad says <u>The Pit and the Pendulum</u> is a scary story.

6. The "Philadelphia Inquirer" is delivered daily.

The <u>Philadelphia Inquirer</u> is delivered daily.

✓ Write the following titles correctly. The words in ( ) tell you what they are.

7. the life you save may be your own (story)

8. i want a hippopotamus for christmas (song)

9. the lion, the witch, and the wardrobe (book)

10. stopping by woods on a snowy evening (poem)

11. ottawa citizen (newspaper)

12. sports illustrated for kids (magazine)

13. this is just to say (poem)

14. riding the elevator into the sky (poem)

Topic Sentences

All the sentences in a paragraph should tell about one main idea. Often the main idea is stated in a **topic sentence.** This sentence may appear anywhere in the paragraph, but it is often the first sentence.

Write the letter of a topic sentence (A, B, C) that fits each group of details (1, 2, 3).

A Running is good for you.

B Training for a marathon requires months of work.

C A wide range of running clothes is available.

1. Short distances at first

Work up to longer distances

Training varied with swimming and bicycling

2. Reflective vests for safety at night

Shoes with special support

New fabrics that "breathe" for comfort

3. Development of strong muscles

Improved circulation of blood

Relaxing for the mind

Invent a name for the athlete described below. Write a topic sentence about him or her based on the details.

Ran one of the fastest marathons in the world last year

Born into a very poor family and became a doctor

Informational Article

An **informational article** gives readers facts about a topic. The writer may be an expert in the subject or a student like you who has researched the subject. An effective informational article presents facts in a way that is easy for the nonexpert reader to understand.

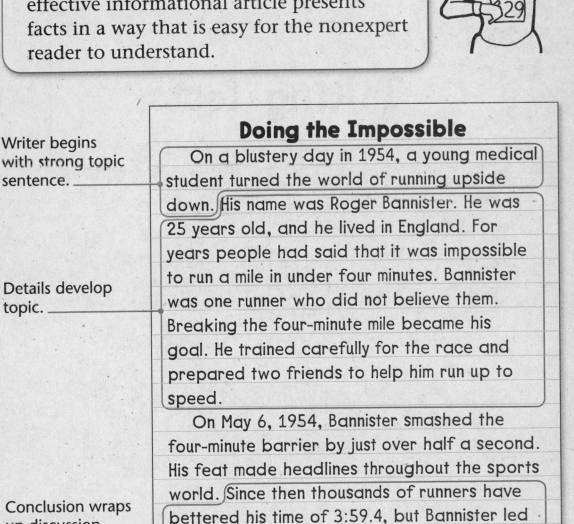

Writer begins with strong topic sentence.

Details develop topic.

Conclusion wraps up discussion.

Doing the Impossible

On a blustery day in 1954, a young medical student turned the world of running upside down. His name was Roger Bannister. He was 25 years old, and he lived in England. For years people had said that it was impossible to run a mile in under four minutes. Bannister was one runner who did not believe them. Breaking the four-minute mile became his goal. He trained carefully for the race and prepared two friends to help him run up to speed.

On May 6, 1954, Bannister smashed the four-minute barrier by just over half a second. His feat made headlines throughout the sports world. Since then thousands of runners have bettered his time of 3:59.4, but Bannister led the way.

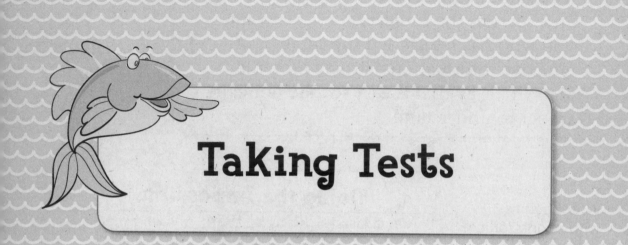

Taking Tests

Follow these tips when writing for a test:

Before Writing

- Read the prompt carefully. What does it ask you to do?
- Write down key words that name your audience *(warn <u>people who eat junk food</u>)*, state the purpose of the composition *(<u>give directions</u>)*, and tell you how to organize your points *(provide <u>step-by-step instructions</u>)*.
- Use a graphic organizer to plan your composition.
- Determine the tone of your writing (friendly, formal).

During Writing

- Reread the prompt as you write to make sure you are on topic.
- Keep in mind your graphic organizer and stay focused.
- Write a good beginning. You might engage readers with a thought-provoking question or an interesting fact.
- Develop and elaborate ideas. Support your main idea, your observations, or your opinion.
- Write a strong ending. Try to write a "clincher" sentence to provide a clear ending. You might add a final comment of your own or challenge your reader with a command.

After Writing

- Check your grammar and mechanics (punctuation, spelling).
- Reread the prompt and review your work. There's still time to add words or correct errors.

Writing a Personal Narrative

A **test** may ask you to write a personal narrative. Your narrative should have a beginning, middle, and end. Use words such as *once* and *now* to show the order of events. Follow the tips below.

Understand the prompt.   Read the prompt carefully. A test prompt for a personal narrative could look like this:

Think about an exciting experience or event in your life. Write a personal narrative about it.

Key words: *experience, event in your life, personal narrative.*

Find a good topic.   Get ideas from photos and diaries.

Organize your ideas.   Write notes on scratch paper.

Event Kite flying
What Happened?   went kite flying with Amy and Mom
When   last Saturday   **Where**   the park
Beginning   My mom agreed to take me to fly a kite.
Middle   The kite got caught in a tree.
End   Mom said she would get me another kite.

Write a good beginning   Write a snappy first sentence.

Develop and elaborate ideas.   Use your notes.

Write a strong ending.   Describe how you felt.

Check your work.   Add vivid words.

See how the personal narrative below addresses the prompt, flows from the beginning to the middle to the end, and strongly expresses the writer's voice.

1 —

2 —

3 —

2 —

Last Saturday was a perfect warm, windy day to fly a kite! I just couldn't wait to get to the park. Mom agreed to take me there, along with my best friend, Amy.

After we got to the park, Amy held the kite high. Then she let it go as I began running wildly. The kite darted around as I furiously unrolled the string. Then the wind lifted the kite. It almost seemed like the kite could touch the clouds.

Amy wanted to fly the kite, and I gave her the string. At first, she was smiling as the kite sailed through the sky. Suddenly, the wind died down, and the kite began to dive. Then the kite got caught in a tree. Amy looked really sad, but I told her not to worry. I could get a new kite, but good friends are much harder to get.

4 —

5 —

1. The first sentence sets the scene.

2. Vivid words strengthen the writer's voice.

3. The writer clearly shows the order of events.

4. Compound sentences make the writing more interesting.

5. The ending shows the writer's feelings about friendship.

Writing a How-to Report

A **test** may ask you to explain how to do something. Include all the steps. Use words such as *first* and *finally* to show the order of steps. Follow the tips below.

Understand the prompt.   Read the prompt carefully. A prompt for a how-to explanation could look like this:

Write a report that tells how to make or do something. Make your report interesting to read and easy to understand. Explain all the steps and materials needed.

Key words: *report, how to, steps and materials*.

Find a good topic.   Think of things that you have done. Choose a topic that you can explain in a few simple steps.

Organize your ideas.   Make a how-to chart.

TASK	STEPS
Searching the Internet	1. Turn on computer.
	2. Connect to Internet.
	3. Type in topic words.

Write a good beginning.   Write a strong topic sentence.

Develop and elaborate ideas.   Focus your writing. Include words such as *first* and *then* to show order.

Write a strong ending.   Sum up your ideas.

Check your work.   Share your work with a classmate to get ideas and suggestions on how to improve your report.

See how the report below addresses the prompt, has a strong beginning and end, and stays focused on the topic.

1 —

    Have you ever needed to find information quickly? The Internet is a great way to get facts fast. You'll need a computer with access to the Internet. Use a modem or even DSL, which is a type of high-speed connection to the Internet.

    Of course, the first thing you do is turn on the computer. Then connect it to the Internet and log on to a search engine, such as Google. Now, type a word or words about your topic into the search box. Specific words can help narrow your search. If you type a general word, such as *dog*, you will get a million responses. Finally, visit links that the search engine gives you. Now you have information at your fingertips.

4

2 —

3

5

1. This question engages the reader.

2. The writer uses words that show the order of steps.

3. Strong adjectives make the information clear.

4. Special terms are defined.

5. This strong ending sums up the writer's purpose.

Writing a Compare/Contrast Essay

A **test** may ask you to write a compare/contrast essay. Choose subjects that are alike and different. Use words to show likenesses (*and*, *also*) and differences (*however*, *but*). Follow the tips below.

Understand the prompt.   A prompt for a compare/contrast essay could look like this:

> Write an essay comparing and contrasting two foods you would find in a school cafeteria.

Key words and phrases are *essay*, *comparing and contrasting*, and *foods*.

Find a good topic.   List things that you could compare. Write the qualities of each item. Narrow your list to subjects that can be compared *and* contrasted.

Organize your ideas.   Make a compare/contrast organizer on scratch paper, like the one below.

Food: Carrots Crunchy and bitter Long and orange Vegetable	**Food:** Peas Soft and sweet Round and green Vegetable

Write a good beginning.   Write a strong topic sentence that presents your idea and grabs your reader's attention.

Develop and elaborate ideas.   Use your compare/ contrast organizer to help you focus your writing. Begin by describing likenesses and then move on to differences.

Write a strong ending.   Make a clear statement.

Check your work.   Share your essay with a classmate.

See how the essay below addresses the prompt, has a strong beginning and end, and stays focused on the topic.

1 — How do you feel about peas and carrots? Even if you don't like them, it is interesting to see how they are alike and different. Peas and carrots are similar because they are both vegetables. They are also both good for you.

2 — Even though peas and carrots do not taste the same, I like to eat them both. Peas are soft and sweet, but carrots are crunchy and slightly bitter. Peas and carrots look different too. Peas are round and green. However, carrots are long and orange. Even though these vegetables are different in some ways, I love to eat them both.

4

3

5

1. The first sentence poses a question to readers.

2. Words such as *crunchy* and *bitter* appeal to the senses.

3. The writer knows of subject-verb agreement.

4. Key words are used to show a clear contrast.

5. This strong ending sums up the writer's thoughts.

Writing a Story

A **test** may ask you to write a story. Use vivid verbs and exact nouns and adjectives. Remember that dialogue—the words people say—makes your story seem real. Follow the tips below.

Understand the prompt.   Read the prompt carefully. A test prompt for a story could look like this:

> Write a story about a mystery that takes place in a school. Include at least two characters and dialogue.

Key words and phrases are *story*, *mystery*, and *school*.

Find a good topic.   List mysterious things that might happen in a school. Think of the characters and what they might do or say. Then narrow your list.

Organize your ideas.   Make a story chart.

Story Chart
Title   "The Thief"
Characters   Paul, a student, and Ms. Crosby, his teacher
Mystery   Who stole a gold pen from the desk?
Solution   A crow stole the pen.

Write a good beginning.   Write a strong opening sentence that catches your reader's attention.

Develop and elaborate ideas. Use your story organizer as an outline for your ideas.

Write a strong ending. Leave your reader satisfied.

Check your work. Share your story with a classmate to see what he or she thinks could be added or left out.

See how the story below addresses the prompt.

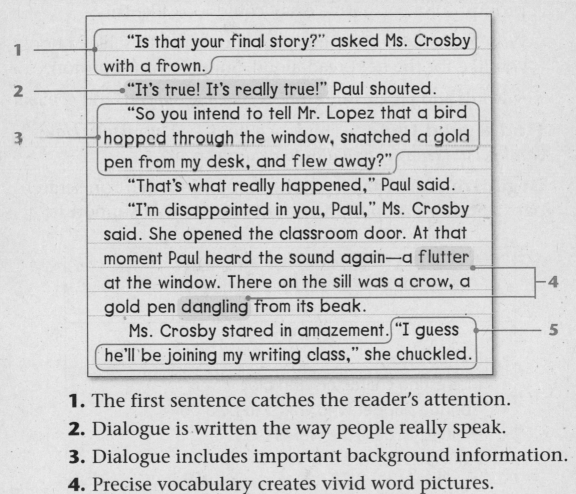

1   "Is that your final story?" asked Ms. Crosby with a frown.

2   "It's true! It's really true!" Paul shouted.

3   "So you intend to tell Mr. Lopez that a bird hopped through the window, snatched a gold pen from my desk, and flew away?"

"That's what really happened," Paul said.

"I'm disappointed in you, Paul," Ms. Crosby said. She opened the classroom door. At that moment Paul heard the sound again—a flutter at the window. There on the sill was a crow, a gold pen dangling from its beak. 4

Ms. Crosby stared in amazement. "I guess he'll be joining my writing class," she chuckled. 5

1. The first sentence catches the reader's attention.

2. Dialogue is written the way people really speak.

3. Dialogue includes important background information.

4. Precise vocabulary creates vivid word pictures.

5. The ending introduces a touch of humor.

Writing a Persuasive Essay

A **test** may ask you to write a persuasive essay. Support your opinion with reasons and use words such as *should* and *best*. Follow the tips below.

Understand the prompt.   Read the prompt carefully. A prompt for a persuasive essay could look like this:

> Write an essay persuading your classmates to select a book you like for the next read-aloud. Support your opinion.

Key words and phrases are *essay, persuading, support,* and *opinion.*

Find a good topic.   Think of a book. Ask yourself: *How can I persuade my classmates to read this book?*

Organize your ideas.   Write an opinion chart on scratch paper. State your opinion and list reasons that support it.

STATEMENT OF OPINION
I think we should read *Pinocchio* for the next class read-aloud.
REASONS
• Famous story
• Interesting characters and plot
• About a puppet who wants to be a boy
• Exciting to hear the words read
• Pinocchio has dreams

Write a good beginning.   Write a strong topic sentence that expresses your opinion.

Develop and elaborate ideas. Use the chart to review your reasons. Decide which reason is most important.

Write a strong ending. "Wrap up" your essay.

Check your work. Make any necessary changes.

See how the persuasive essay below addresses the prompt, has a strong beginning and end, and stays focused on the topic.

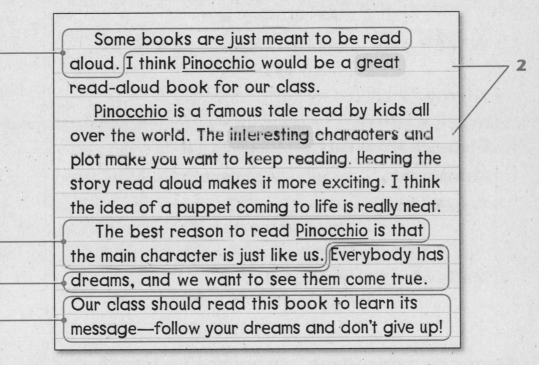

> Some books are just meant to be read aloud. I think Pinocchio would be a great read-aloud book for our class.
>
> Pinocchio is a famous tale read by kids all over the world. The interesting characters and plot make you want to keep reading. Hearing the story read aloud makes it more exciting. I think the idea of a puppet coming to life is really neat.
>
> The best reason to read Pinocchio is that the main character is just like us. Everybody has dreams, and we want to see them come true.
>
> Our class should read this book to learn its message—follow your dreams and don't give up!

1. The first sentence makes the reader want to know more.

2. The writer uses persuasive words effectively.

3. Argument builds to the most important reason.

4. A compound sentence makes the writing flow smoothly.

5. This strong ending sums up the writer's thoughts.

Writing a Summary

A **test** may ask you to summarize information from a time line, diagram, or chart. You will need to read the information carefully and shape it into your own sentences. Follow the tips below.

About the Sun

What it does   Supplies heat and light to Earth
Makes life possible

Energy   Produced by nuclear fusion
Travels in waves of particles called photons

Distance from Earth   About 93 million miles

Movement   Spins around center of Milky Way galaxy

Type of body   Large star
One of more than 100 billion stars in galaxy

Made of   Hot gases
75% hydrogen, 25% helium

Organize your ideas.   In a time line, information will already be arranged in order. With a chart or diagram, you will need to decide how to present information. In any case, you must put words into complete sentences and provide a beginning and a conclusion.

Write a good beginning.   You might engage readers with a thought-provoking question.

Develop and elaborate ideas. Include all important details from the chart. Make sure the details support your main idea.

Write a strong ending. Try to write a "clincher" sentence. You might add a final comment of your own.

Check your work. Are there places that need more details or clearer information?

See how the summary below is based on information from the chart, along with the writer's own comment and sentences.

1 —— Could there be life on Earth without the sun? The answer is no. The energy that makes life
2 —— possible all comes from the sun. This heat and light energy travels in the form of photons. These are waves of particles produced by —— 3 nuclear fusion on the sun.

This energy comes from 93 million miles away. That's how far the sun is from Earth. Where exactly is the sun? The sun is the closest star to Earth. It is made of hot gases—75% hydrogen
4 —— and 25% helium. Imagine all that energy from a —— 5 ball of gases 93 million miles away!

1. The opening question grabs the reader's attention.

2. This sentence states the main idea.

3. The writer explains a technical term.

4. Use of the pronoun *it* avoids repeating *the sun*.

5. This ending reveals the writer's voice.

Grammar Patrol

Grammar Patrol

adjective An adjective describes a noun or a pronoun.

> Ponds are *active* places.
> *Several* chipmunks run through the *wet* grass.

Adjectives have two different forms that are used to make comparisons.

- Use the *–er* form of an adjective to compare two persons, places, or things.

  > Frogs have *smoother* skin than toads.

- Use the *–est* form of an adjective to compare three or more persons, places, or things.

  > Snails are the *slowest* pond creatures.

- The words *more* and *most* are often used with adjectives of two or more syllables to make comparisons.

  > The ducks were *more comical* than usual.
  > The goose is the *most common* bird here.

- Some adjectives show comparison in a special way. The correct forms of *good*, *bad*, *much*, and *little* are shown below.

good weather	*better* weather	*best* weather
bad storm	*worse* storm	*worst* storm
much snow	*more* snow	*most* snow
little fog	*less* fog	*least* fog

article The words, *a*, *an*, and *the* are a special kind of adjective. They are called articles. *The* is used with both singular and plural nouns. *A* and *an* are used only with singular nouns.

> *The* animals at *the* pond are very busy.
> *A* friend and I spent *an* afternoon there.

- Use *a* before a word that begins with a consonant sound.

  > *a* beaver   *a* pleasant afternoon

- Use *an* before a word that begins with a vowel sound.

  > *an* owl   *an* underwater plant

adverb   A word that describes a verb is an adverb.

- Some adverbs ask the question "How?"

    The fox hides *slyly* behind the bushes. (how?)

- Some adverbs answer the question "Where?"

    Aesop wrote fables *here*. (where?)

- Other adverbs answer the question "When?"

    Often a fable tells about one event. (when?)

Adverbs can be used to compare actions.

- Use the *–er* form or *more* to compare two actions. Most adverbs that end in *–ly* use *more*.

    The ant worked *harder* than the cricket.
    The tortoise moved *more steadily* than the hare.

- Use the *–est* form or *most* to compare three or more actions. Most adverbs that end in *–ly* use *most*.

    The ant worked *hardest* of all the insects.
    The tortoise moved *most steadily* of all.

The word *not* is an adverb. It means "no." Do not use two words that mean "no" in the same sentence.

    Wrong: It *wouldn't never* matter to me.
    Right: It *wouldn't* ever matter to me.
    Right: It would *never* matter to me.

contraction   A contraction is a shortened form of two words. An apostrophe replaces a letter or letters.

- Some contractions join a pronoun and a verb.

    I have never been in a dairy shed before.
    I've never been in a dairy shed before.

- Some contractions are formed from a verb and the word *not*.

    I *cannot* believe you *did not* bring your banjo.
    I *can't* believe you *didn't* bring your banjo.

noun A noun names a person, place, or thing.

The *settlers* came to *America* on a *ship*.
(person)   (place)   (thing)

A **singular noun** names one person, place, or thing.

The *settler* kept the *cow* in the *barn*.

A **plural noun** names more than one person, place, or thing.

The *settlers* kept their *cows* in their *barns*.

- Add -*s* to form the plural of most nouns.

  colonist*s*   river*s*   pea*s*   chicken*s*

- Add -*es* to form the plural of nouns that end in *ch*, *sh*, *s*, *ss*, *x*, or *z*.

  bench*es*   bush*es*   bus*es*   box*es*

- If a noun ends in a consonant and *y*, change *y* to *i* and add -*es* to form the plural.

  Singular: library   city   cherry
  Plural: librar*ies*   cit*ies*   cherr*ies*

- Some plurals are formed by changing the spelling of the singular noun.

  Singular: man   child   foot   mouse
  Plural: m*en*   child*ren*   f*ee*t   m*i*ce

- A few nouns have the same singular and plural forms.

  Singular: elk   moose   deer   sheep
  Plural: elk   moose   deer   sheep

A **common noun** names any person, place, or thing.

A *colonist* founded the *town*.

A **proper noun** names a particular person, place, or thing.

William Penn founded *Philadelphia*.

A **possessive noun** shows ownership.

* To form the possessive of a singular noun, add an apostrophe and *s* (*'s*) to the singular noun.

  Ben Franklin's many talents amazed people.

* To form the possessive of a plural noun ending in *s*, add an apostrophe (*s'*).

  shoemakers' hammers   *blacksmiths'* forges

* To form the possessive of a plural noun that does not end in *s*, add an apostrophe and *s* (*'s*).

  men's hats   *mice's* tails   two *deer's* tracks

preposition   A preposition is a word that shows how a noun or pronoun is related to other words in the same sentence.

  We sing *in* the car.

A preposition begins a group of words called a **prepositional phrase**. At the end of the phrase is a noun or pronoun called the **object of the preposition**.

  Preposition: The dog buried its bone *in* the yard.
  Prepositional phrase: *in the yard*
  Object of the proposition: *yard*

pronoun   A pronoun takes the place of a noun or nouns.

  Nouns: *Linda* writes *poems*.
  Pronouns: *She* enjoys writing *them*.

The pronouns *I, you, she, he, it, we,* and *they* are **subject pronouns**. Use these pronouns to replace nouns that are the subjects of sentences.

  Robert Frost had been a teacher and a farmer.
  He wrote many poems about nature.

The pronouns *me, you, him, her, it, us* and *them* are **object pronouns**. You can use these pronouns to replace nouns in the predicate of a sentence.

> Paul read *poems* to *Jill*.
> Paul read *them* to *her*.

The pronouns *my, your, his, her, its, our,* and *their* are **possessive pronouns**. A possessive pronoun shows ownership. Possessive pronouns can replace nouns.

> That *writer's* home is in the mountains.
> *Her* poems usually involve nature.

sentence   A sentence is a group of words that expresses a complete thought.

> *People of all ages enjoy hobbies.*

A **declarative sentence** makes a statement. It ends with a period (.).

> *Hobbies are important in people's lives.*

An **interrogative sentence** asks a question. It ends with a question mark (?).

> *What is your hobby?*

An **imperative sentence** gives a command or makes a request. It usually ends with a period (.).

> *Please get your kite ready.*   *Come to our party!*

An **exclamatory sentence** expresses strong feeling. It ends with an exclamation mark (!).

> *That kite will crash!*   *How happy I am!*

A **simple sentence** has one subject and one predicate. It expresses one complete thought.

> *Kites come in many different shapes.*

A **compound sentence** contains two simple sentences joined by the word *and, but,* or *or*. Use a comma in a compound sentence before the word *and, but,* or *or*.

The day was cool, and *clouds drifted across the sun.*

subject and predicate The subject is the part of the sentence that names someone or something. The predicate tells what the subject is or does. Both the subject and the predicate may be one word or many words.

Currents/move ocean water around the world.
The most common mineral/is salt.
Ocean water/moves.
Sea water/flows in vast streams.

The **simple subject** is the main word in the complete subject.

The five biggest *oceans* are really one huge ocean.

A sentence may have more than one simple subject. The word *and* may be used to join simple subjects, making a **compound subject**. The simple subjects share the same predicate.

Spiny *crabs* and colorful *fish* scurry along the underwater reef.

The **simple predicate** is the main word or words in the complete predicate.

Ocean waters *flow* in vast streams.

A sentence may have more than one simple predicate. The word *and* may be used to join simple predicates, making a **compound predicate**. The simple predicates share the same subject.

Some worms *live* and *feed* in the ocean.

verb A verb is a word that shows action or being.

Nina *paints* in art class. (action)
That picture *is* beautiful. (being)

An **action verb** shows action. It tells what the subject of a sentence does.

> The art teacher *welcomed* the students.

A verb can be more than one word. The **main verb** is the most important verb. A **helping verb** works with the main verb.

> Many people have *admired* Picasso's paintings. (main verb)
> His name *is* known all over the world. (helping verb)

A **linking verb** shows being. It tells what the subject is or was.

> Grandma Moses *was* a famous artist.

When the correct subject and verb are used together, we say they agree. The form of the linking verb *be* that is used depends on the subject of the sentence. Study the following chart.

Using the Forms of *be*

Use *am* and *was*	with *I*
Use *is* and *was*	with *she, he, it,* and singular nouns
Use *are* and *were*	with *we, you, they,* and plural nouns

The **tense** of a verb shows the time of the action.

A verb in the **present tense** shows action that happens now.

> Eli *forms* the tiles.

A verb in the present tense must agree with the subject of the sentence.

- With *he, she, it,* or a singular noun, add *-s* or *-es* to the verb.
  > The student learn*s*.   My cousin teach*es*.   He walk*s*.

- If a verb ends in *ch, sh, s, ss, x,* or *z,* add *-es*. Notice the word *teaches* above.

- With *I, you, we, they,* or a plural noun, do not add *-s* or *-es*.
  > The students learn.   My cousins teach.   They walk.

A verb in the **future tense** shows action that will happen. The future tense is formed with the helping verb *will*.

> Ann *will create* a vase.

A verb in the **past tense** shows action that already happened.

Lee *washed* pots.

The past tenses of irregular verbs are not formed by adding *-ed*. Some irregular verbs are shown in the following chart.

Verb	Past	Past with *have, has,* or *had*
begin	began	begun
bring	brought	brought
come	came	come
do	did	done
eat	ate	eaten
fall	fell	fallen
find	found	found
fly	flew	flown
give	gave	given
go	went	gone
grow	grew	grown
ride	rode	ridden
run	ran	run
see	saw	seen
take	took	taken
throw	threw	thrown
write	wrote	written

The spelling of some verbs changes when *-es* or *-ed* is added.

- If a verb ends in a consonant and *y*, change the *y* to *i* before adding *-es* or *-ed*.

  study   stud*ies*   stud*ied*

- If a verb ends in one vowel and one consonant, double the final consonant before adding *-ed*.

  trap   tra*pped*   stir   sti*rred*

Capitalization

first word of a sentence   Every sentence begins with a capital letter.

> *People* enjoy having special projects.

proper noun   Each important word in a proper noun begins with a capital letter.

- Capitalize each word in the name of a person or pet.

    > *Patrice Gomez* owns a cat named *Duke*.

- Capitalize an initial in a name. Put a period after the initial.

    > William *L.* Chen is a doctor in our neighborhood.

- Capitalize a title before a name. If the title is an *abbreviation* (a shortened form of a word), put a period after it.

    > *President* Jefferson   *Dr.* Jonas Salk

- Capitalize every important word in the names of particular places or things.

    > *Statue of Liberty*   *Ellis Island*   *New York Harbor*

- Capitalize names of days, months, holidays, and special days.

    > *Tuesday*   *April*   *Fourth of July*

pronoun *I*   The pronoun *I* is always capitalized.

> May *I* go skating this afternoon?

letter   Capitalize the first word of the greeting and the first word of the closing of a letter.

> *Dear* Mother,   *Dear* Sir: *Sincerely* yours,

title of books, movies, songs, and other works   Capitalize the first word, the last word, and all of the important words in the title of works.

> The Secret Life of Harold the Bird Watcher
> "The Star Spangled Banner"

quotation   Begin the first word in a quotation with a capital letter.

    The Hare asked, *"How about a race?"*

Punctuation

period   Declarative sentences and imperative sentences end with a period (.).

    I stood on the corner.   *Wait for the signal.*

- Put a period after an initial in a name.

    J. P. Jones   *Abigail S. Adams*

- Put a period after an abbreviation (a shortened form of a word).

    Mr.   *Mrs.*   *Ms.*   *Dr.*

question mark   An interrogative sentence ends with a question mark (?).

    Do you have more than one hobby?

exclamation mark   An exclamatory sentence ends with an exclamation mark (!).

    That kite will crash!

comma   A comma (,) is a signal that tells a reader to pause.

- Use a comma after *yes*, *no*, or *well* at the beginning of a sentence.

    Yes, I saw the display of Eskimo art.
    Well, my favorites were the bears made of silver.

- Use a comma to set off the name of the person spoken to.

    Your painting is very beautiful, Roberta.

- Use a comma to separate words in a series. A series is made up of three or more items. No comma is used after the last word in the series. The last comma goes before the word *and*.

    The artists carve, smooth, and polish their work.

- Use a comma to separate the city from the state.

  I grew up in *Tulsa, Oklahoma.*

- Use a comma to separate the day and the year.

  Pablo was born on *February 7, 2000.*

- Use a comma after the greeting of a friendly letter. Use a comma after the closing of a friendly or a business letter.

  Dear Kim,   Your friend,   Yours truly,

- Use a comma before the word *and*, *but*, or *or* in a compound sentence.

  The merchants crossed central Asia, and they reached China.

quotation marks   A quotation is the exact words someone speaks. Quotation marks (" ") show where a speaker's exact words begin and end.

- Use quotation marks before and after a quotation. Begin the first word in a quotation with a capital letter. When the quotation comes last, use a comma to separate the speaker from the quotation.

  The Tortoise said, "I'm not going to lose this race."

- When the quotation comes first, use a comma, a question mark, or an exclamation mark to separate the quotation from the speaker. The end mark of a quotation always comes just before the second quotation mark. Put a period at the end of the sentence.

  Statement: "Let's do something else," replied the Tortoise.
  Question: "Are you afraid you'll lose?" teased the Hare.
  Exclamation: "I'm not afraid!" snapped the Tortoise.

- Enclose the titles of stories, songs, poems, and articles in quotation marks.

  Story: "The Use of Force"
  Song: "Of Thee I Sing"
  Poem: "Dear March, Come In!"
  Article: "Let's Make Music"

Underline the titles of newspapers, magazines, books, plays, and movies.

In materials you read, these titles are printed in italics.

Newspaper: <u>Denver Post</u>
Magazine: <u>Popular Mechanics</u>
Book: <u>A Wind in the Door</u>
Play: <u>Man of La Mancha</u>
Movie: <u>Invaders from Mars</u>

apostrophe   Use an apostrophe (') to show where a letter or letters have been left out in a *contraction* (a shortened form of two words).

we'd (we + had)   *wasn't* (was + not)

• Use an apostrophe to form the possessive of a noun.

man's   *James's*   *men's*   *workers'*

colon   Use a colon (:) after the greeting in a business letter.

Dear Mr. Kurtz: *Dear Sir or Madam:*

Frequently Misspelled Words

a lot
afraid
again
almost
already
always
another
are
athlete
basketball
beautiful
because
before
believe
brother
brought
buy
caught
chocolate
Christmas
clothes
control
could
cousin
Dad's
decided
didn't
different
disappear
doesn't
don't
enough
especially
everybody
everyone

everything
except
excited
family
favorite
February
field
finally
first
found
friend
getting
government
grabbed
happened
heard
hero
his
hospital
house
I
I'm
instead
into
it's
knew
know
knowledge
let's
library
little
maybe
might
minute
Mom

morning
myself
of
off
once
one
opened
our
outside
people
piece
presents
pretty
probably
radio
really
right
said
scared
school
separate
should
since
sincerely
something
sometimes
special
started
stopped
successful
sure
surprised
swimming
that's
their

then
there
they
they're
thought
through
to
too
took
tries
truly
TV
two
until
upon
usually
vacation
very
want
was
watch
weird
we're
were
what
when
where
which
who
whole
with
would
you're

D'Nealian™ Alphabet

a b c d e f g h i

j k l m n o p q r s t

u v w x y z

A B C D E F G

H I J K L M N O

P Q R S T U V

W X Y Z . , ' ?

1 2 3 4 5 6

7 8 9 10

Manuscript Alphabet

a b c d e f g

h i j k l m n

o p q r s t u

v w x y z

A B C D E F G

H I J K L M N

O P Q R S T U

V W X Y Z , ' . ?

1 2 3 4 5 6

7 8 9 10

a b c d e f g

h i j k l m m n

o p q r s t u

v w x y z

A B C D E F G

H I J K L M N

O P 2 R S T U

V W X Y Z . , ' ?

1 2 3 4 5 6

7 8 9 10

Index

T

Tenses, 128–131
Test preparation, 52, 58, 64, 70, 76, 82, 88, 94, 100, 106, 112, 118, 124, 130, 136, 142, 148, 154, 160, 166, 172, 178, 184, 190, 196, 202, 208, 214, 220, 226
Tests. *See* Writing for tests.
Time-order words. *See* Writing.
Titles
  of books, magazines, newspapers, 224–227
  of people, 206–209
  of stories, poems, songs, 224–227

V

Verb phrases. *See* Verbs.
Verbs, 250–252
  action, 110–113
  agreement, 122–125
  be, 110–113
  future tense, 128–131
  helping, 116–119
  irregular, 134–137
  is, am, are, was, were, 110–113
  linking, 110–113
  main, 116–119
  past tense, 128–131
  phrases, 116–119
  present tense, 128–131
Voice. *See* Writing.

W

Word choice. *See* Writing.
Writer's craft. *See topics under* Writing. *See also main entries.*
Writing
  conventions, 22–25
  details, 96, 120, 150, 222
  dialogue, 138
  elaboration, 156
  eliminate wordiness, 168
  exact words, 180
  figurative language, 84
  focus/ideas, 2–5, 186
  good beginnings, 144
  good conclusions, 216
  include necessary information, 90
  know audience, 192
  main idea, 2–3
  models, 4–5, 8–9, 12–13, 16–17, 20–21, 24–25, 27–30, 32–35, 37–40, 42–45, 233, 235, 237, 239, 241, 243
  biography, 205
  book or story review, 175